Quilt A COLORFUL CHRISTMAS™

EDITED BY JEANNE STAUFFER AND SANDRA L. HATCH

HOUSE of
WHITE
BIRCHES

PUBLISHERS
SINCE 1947

Quilt a Colorful Christmas

EDITORS	Jeanne Stauffer, Sandra L. Hatch
ART DIRECTOR	Brad Snow
PUBLISHING SERVICES MANAGER	Brenda Gallmeyer
ASSOCIATE EDITOR	Dianne Schmidt
ASSISTANT ART DIRECTOR	Nick Pierce
COPY SUPERVISOR	Michelle Beck
COPY EDITORS	Sue Harvey, Nicki Lehman, Beverly Richardson
TECHNICAL ARTIST	Connie Rand
GRAPHIC ARTS SUPERVISOR	Ronda Bechinski
BOOK DESIGN	Amy Lin
GRAPHIC ARTISTS	Debby Keel, Edith Teegarden
PRODUCTION ASSISTANTS	Cheryl Kempf, Marj Morgan
PHOTOGRAPHY	Tammy Christian, Carl Clark, Christena Green, Matthew Owen
PHOTO STYLIST	Tammy Nussbaum
CHIEF EXECUTIVE OFFICER	John Robinson
PUBLISHING DIRECTOR	David J. McKee
EDITORIAL DIRECTOR	Vivian Rothe
BOOK MARKETING DIRECTOR	Craig Scott

Printed in China
First Printing: 2005
Library of Congress Number: 2004116655
Hardcover ISBN: 1-59217-073-0
Softcover ISBN: 1-59217-074-9

Welcome

What could be better than Christmas and quilting, all rolled up in one book? Christmas is such a special time of the year, full of excitement, color and joy. It's a great time for showing family, friends, neighbors and co-workers that you care about them.

Quilting does the same thing for us throughout the year! There is the excitement of starting a new quilt. From the beginning when we select the fabric to the end when we stitch on a label, every step of the way, quilting brings joy and comfort. Once the quilt is completed, it is a time of sharing and caring for others as you give the quilt to someone you love or use it to enrich your own life by hanging it on a wall or placing it on a bed to decorate your home.

Christmas is so much like quilting. With each step you complete in making a quilt, it's like slowly opening a Christmas present until at last you see the gift or the completed quilt. Each step along the way is just as much fun and brings just as much pleasure as the final step does.

We've selected some great designs for this book that we know you will love. So begin Christmas now by selecting the first design you want to make. The joy and color of Christmas are waiting for you inside the pages of this book!

Warm regards,

Jeanne Stauffer

Sandra L. Hatch

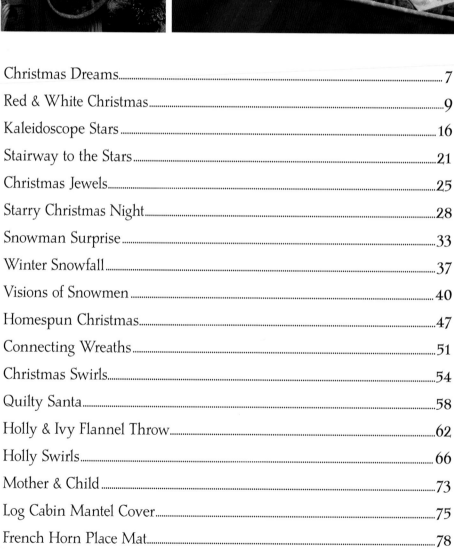

Contents

DESIGN BY **LUCY A. FAZELY & MICHAEL L. BURNS**

Christmas Dreams

Fused squares create quick-stitched blocks in a holiday bed quilt.

Project Specifications

Skill Level: Beginner
Quilt Size: 69" x 82"
Block Size: 12" x 12"
Number of Blocks: 20

Materials

- ⅞ yard red tonal check
- ⅞ yard green/black print
- 1⅝ yards cream print
- 1⅝ yards red print
- 2 yards poinsettia print
- Backing 75" x 88"
- Batting 75" x 88"
- All-purpose thread to match fabrics
- Clear nylon monofilament
- Quilting thread
- ⅔ yard 12"-wide fusible web
- Quilt basting spray
- Basic sewing tools and supplies

Cutting

Step 1. Cut four 6½" by fabric width strips cream print for A.

Step 2. Cut four 6½" by fabric width strips red print for B-C units.

Step 3. Cut eight 3½" by fabric width strips red print for A-B units.

Step 4. Cut eight 3½" by fabric width strips cream print for C.

Step 5. Cut one 6" by fabric width strip green/black print for D.

Step 6. Cut two 12½" by fabric width strips red tonal check; subcut strips into (49) 1½" E strips.

Step 7. Cut two 1½" by fabric width strips green/black print; subcut into (30) 1½" F squares.

Step 8. Cut six 2½" by fabric width strips green/black print. Join strips on short ends to make one long strip; subcut into two 66½" G and two 57½" H strips.

Step 9. Cut seven 6½" by fabric width strips poinsettia print. Join strips on short ends to make one long strip; subcut into two 70½" I strips and two 69½" J strips.

Step 10. Cut eight 2¼" by fabric width strips poinsettia print for binding.

Christmas Dreams
12" x 12" Block

Making Blocks

Step 1. Sew a 3½"-wide B strip to each side of an A strip; press seams toward B. Repeat for four strip sets.

Step 2. Subcut the A-B strip sets into (20) 6½" A-B units as shown in Figure 1.

Figure 1
Subcut the A-B strip sets
into 6½" A-B units.

Step 3. Sew a C strip to each side of a 6½"-wide B strip; press seams toward B. Repeat for four strip sets.

Step 4. Subcut the B-C strip sets into (40) 3½" B-C units as shown in Figure 2.

Figure 2
Subcut the B-C strip sets
into 3½" B-C units.

Step 5. Sew a B-C unit to opposite sides of an A-B unit as shown in Figure 3; press seams toward B-C units. Repeat to complete 20 A-B-C units.

Figure 3
Sew a B-C unit
to opposite sides
of an A-B unit.

Step 6. Cut the fusible web into one 2" x 5½" rectangle and two 5½" x 20" rectangles. Lightly press each rectangle to the wrong side of the D strip. Cut the fused strip into (80) 1½" x 1½" D squares.

Step 7. Place a D square diagonally over the seam intersections of the pieced A-B-C units as shown in Figure 4; fuse in place.

Figure 4
Place a D square
diagonally over the seam
intersections of the
pieced A-B-C unit.

Step 8. Using clear nylon monofilament or thread to match D, machine-stitch the D pieces in place to complete 20 blocks.

Completing the Top

Step 1. Join four blocks with five E strips to make a row; repeat for five rows. Press seams toward E.

Step 2. Join four E strips with five F squares to make a sashing row; press seams toward E. Repeat for six sashing rows.

Step 3. Join the block rows with the sashing rows to complete the pieced center; press seams toward sashing rows.

Step 4. Sew a G strip to opposite long sides and an H strip to the top and bottom of the pieced center; press seams toward strips.

Step 5. Sew an I strip to opposite long sides and a J strip to the top and bottom of the pieced center; press seams toward strips to complete the top.

Finishing the Quilt

Step 1. Spray backing and top layers with basting spray as directed on product can. Sandwich the batting between the completed top and prepared backing; adjust as necessary to make flat.

Step 2. Hand- or machine-quilt as desired. When quilting is complete, trim batting and backing even with top.

Step 3. Join the binding strips on short ends to make one long strip. Fold the strip in half along length with wrong sides together; press.

Step 4. Sew binding to quilt edges, mitering corners and overlapping ends. Fold binding to the back side and stitch in place. ❋

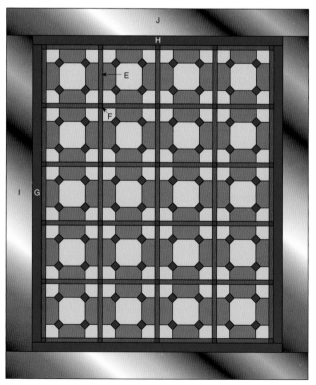

Christmas Dreams
Placement Diagram
69" x 82"

DESIGN BY **BARBARA CLAYTON**

Red & White Christmas

Red on white makes a beautiful visual statement and makes the perfect quilt to decorate your holiday bed.

Project Specifications
Skill Level: Advanced
Quilt Size: 87½" x 101"

Materials
- 4 yards red solid
- 4 yards white solid 96"–98" wide
- Backing 94" x 107"
- Batting 94" x 107"
- Neutral color all-purpose thread
- Clear nylon monofilament
- Red quilting thread
- 7 yards fusible web
- Fray preventative
- 4 (12") squares freezer paper
- Quilter's safety pins
- Fine-point, black indelible marker
- Basic sewing tools and supplies

Cutting
Step 1. Cut a rectangle white solid 71" x 84½" for A quilt center.
Step 2. Cut two 2½" x 84½" B strips and two 2½" x 75" C strips along the length of the red solid.
Step 3. Cut two 7" x 88½" D strips and two 7" x 88" E strips white solid.
Step 4. Cut (10) 2¼" by fabric width strips red solid for binding.

Preparing for Appliqué
Step 1. Referring to Figure 1, mark the A rectangle along the 71" edges as follows: 15¼", 13½", 13½", 13½" and 15¼".

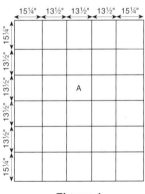

Figure 1
Mark A and press to mark
crease lines as shown.

Step 2. Fold A at each corresponding mark and press four long vertical creases. **Note:** *These creases designate the block areas for appliqué and quilting.*
Step 3. Again referring to Figure 1, mark the A rectangle along the 84½" edges as follows: 15¼", 13½", 13½", 13½", 13½" and 15¼".
Step 4. Fold A at each corresponding mark and press five long horizontal creases, trying to avoid pressing the vertical creases. **Note:** *You should now have 30 pressed areas ready for appliqué.* Set aside.

Step 5. Fold one 12" square of freezer paper in quarters and crease. Unfold and trace the tulip pattern onto one of the creased square sections on the paper using the indelible marker and referring to Figure 2 for positioning of pattern. Repeat on each creased square section to make a complete template; cut out.

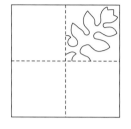 

Figure 2
Trace the tulip pattern onto 1 creased square on the paper.

Figure 3
Trace the feather pattern and hearts onto paper.

Step 6. Repeat with second square of freezer paper to make the feather/heart pattern as shown in Figure 3; set aside.

Step 7. Prepare templates for corner feather, heart and single tulip stem appliqué shapes using patterns given.

Step 8. Trace each template shape onto the paper side of the fusible web as directed on patterns for number to cut.

Step 9. Cut out shapes, leaving a margin around each shape; fuse shapes to red solid. Cut out shapes on marked lines; remove paper backing.

Step 10. Run a thin line of fray preventative along all edges of the appliqué shapes to prevent fraying.

Step 11. Place the feather/heart pattern behind one 15¼" corner square of A with feather shapes 2¾" from the two outside edges and a scant 1" from the two creased lines as shown in Figure 4.

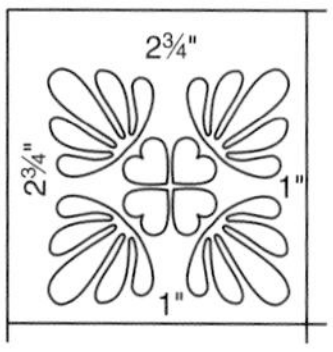

Figure 4
Arrange feather/heart pattern with feather shapes 2¾" from the 2 outside edges and a scant 1" from the 2 creased lines.

Step 12. Arrange four feather shapes on the A piece using pattern as guide for positioning; fuse in place. Arrange four heart shapes in the center of the fused feather design using pattern for positioning of hearts; fuse in place.

Step 13. Repeat to place and fuse a feather/heart design in each A corner. Place a feather/heart design at the center of the top and bottom and two at each side center 2¾" from outside edge and 1" from creased lines referring to the Placement Diagram for positioning.

Step 14. Center and fuse a tulip motif in each of the 12 center creased squares referring to the Placement Diagram for positioning.

Completing the Top

Step 1. Sew a B strip to opposite sides and C strips to the top and bottom of A; press seams toward B and C.

Step 2. Sew a D strip to opposite sides and E strips to the top and bottom of A-B-C; press seams toward B and C.

Step 3. Referring to the Placement Diagram for positioning of all pieces, arrange and fuse four hearts at each corner 1¼" from raw edges and about ½" apart.

Step 4. Place and fuse a single tulip stem on each end of E strips with the tulip angled toward the raw edge, about 3½" to the left of the hearts.

Step 5. Place and fuse another tulip stem 1½" from the first and angled toward C border strips. Repeat with two single tulip stems on each end of the D strips.

Step 6. Place and fuse a heart in the center of each E strip about 2" from C strips. Place one tulip stem on each side of the heart about 1¼" from the heart with the tulip angled toward C.

Step 7. Repeat on each D strip except use three hearts in the center with the two outside hearts 1" from the center heart. Place the tulip stems 2¼" from the center hearts.

Step 8. Roll or fold the fused top, leaving one row free for stitching; use safety pins to hold layers together.

Step 9. Using clear nylon monofilament in the top of the machine and in the bobbin and a medium machine blind-hem stitch, stitch around each fused shape to secure to background. Repeat for all motifs in one row before unpinning, rolling and stitching again to complete all machine appliqué.

Step 10. Trace four feather quilting designs around the edges of a 12" square of freezer paper using the indelible marker, noting that the designs should touch at each corner as shown in Figure 5. Trace the diamond quilting design onto freezer paper.

Figure 5
Trace 4 feather quilting designs onto paper.

Step 11. Referring to Figure 6, draw diagonal lines 1¼" apart in both directions in the center of the feather quilting designs to form a diagonal grid.

Step 12. Transfer the feather quilting design to A referring to the Placement Diagram for positioning and using your favorite transfer method. **Note**: *The black lines should show through the white fabric. If not, a light table is the easiest method of transfer. If you don't have one, you may use a table that pulls apart for leaf inserts with a piece of glass and a light underneath.* The design should be about ¼" from the three pressed creases and 1¼" from the raw edge.

Step 13. Referring to the Placement Diagram for positioning, trace one heart shape at the creased intersections between appliquéd tulip designs; trace the diamond quilting design between the appliquéd tulip designs.

Step 14. Trace feather quilting designs (minus the extra feather on the right end) onto the open spaces of the D and E border strips between the tulip stems 1" from B and C borders, aligning design with the traced feather squares marked on A.

Finishing the Quilt

Step 1. Sandwich the batting between the completed top and prepared backing; pin or baste layers together to hold.

Step 2. Hand-quilt on all marked lines and ¼" from appliquéd motifs using red quilting thread. When quilting is complete, trim batting and backing even with top; remove pins or basting.

Step 3. Lower your machine's feed dogs, attach a darning foot and, using a clear nylon monofilament, free-motion quilt close to the edge around each appliqué shape.

Step 4. Join the binding strips on short ends to make one long strip. Fold the strip in half along length with wrong sides together; press.

Figure 6
Draw diagonal lines 1¼" apart in both directions in the center of the feather quilting designs to form a diagonal grid

Step 5. Sew binding to quilt edges, mitering corners and overlapping ends. Fold binding to the back side and hand- or machine-stitch in place to finish. ❄

Diamond Quilting Design

Red & White Christmas
Placement Diagram
87¹/₂" x 101"

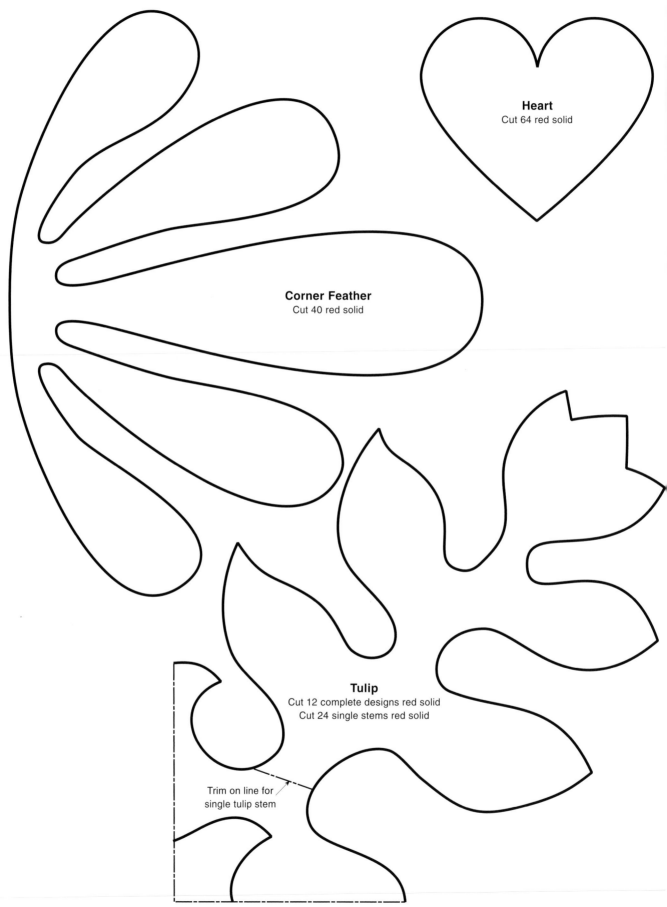

Heart
Cut 64 red solid

Corner Feather
Cut 40 red solid

Tulip
Cut 12 complete designs red solid
Cut 24 single stems red solid

Trim on line for
single tulip stem

Eliminate the extra feather on this end for D & E border quilting design.

Feather Quilting Design

Kaleidoscope Stars

Stitched star-design blocks create a wonderful holiday bed quilt.

Project Specifications

Skill Level: Advanced
Quilt Size: 71" x 86¾"
Block Size: 15¾" x 15¾"
Number of Blocks: 20

Materials

- 1 yard each medium and dark red tonals
- 1⅛ yards medium green print
- 1¼ yards light green swirl
- 1¼ yards tan woven
- 1½ yards cream mottled
- 1⅝ yards dark green tonal
- Backing 77" x 93"
- Batting 77" x 93"
- All-purpose thread to match fabrics
- Clear nylon monofilament
- Quilting thread
- Quilt basting spray
- Basic sewing tools and supplies

Cutting

Step 1. Prepare templates for A/B and E using patterns given.

Step 2. Cut 10 strips each medium (A) and dark red (B) tonals 3" by fabric width. Cut 80 each A and B pieces from strips using the A/B template as shown in Figure 1.

Figure 1
Cut A and B pieces from 3"-wide strips.

Kaleidoscope Star
15¾" x 15¾" Block

Step 3. Cut 14 strips cream mottled 3⅜" by fabric width; subcut strips into (160) 3⅜" C squares. Cut each square on one diagonal to make 320 C triangles.

Step 4. Cut nine 4⅜" by fabric width strips light green swirl; subcut strips into (80) 4⅜" D squares. Cut each square on one diagonal to make 160 D triangles.

Step 5. Cut six 5½" by fabric width strips medium green print; subcut strips into (40) 5½" F squares. Cut each square in half on one diagonal to make 80 F triangles.

Step 6. Cut (20) 1⅞" by fabric width strips tan woven; cut 160 E pieces from strips using the E template as shown in Figure 2.

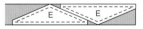

Figure 2
Cut E pieces from 1⅞"-wide strips.

Step 7. Cut eight 4½" by fabric width strips dark green tonal. Join strips on short ends to make one long strip; subcut into two 79¼" G strips and two 71½" H strips.

Step 8. Cut eight 2¼" by fabric width strips dark green tonal for binding.

Making Blocks

Step 1. To complete one Kaleidoscope Star block, sew C to two adjacent sides of one pointed end of four each A and B pieces as shown in Figure 3; press seams toward C.

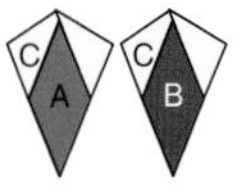

Figure 3
Sew C to 2 adjacent
sides of 1 point of A
and B pieces.

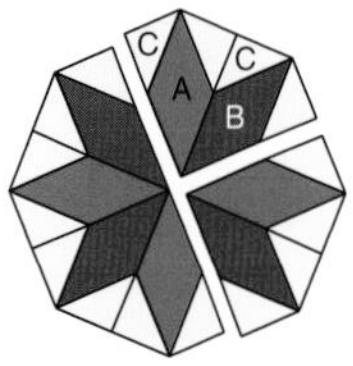

Figure 4
Join units as shown.

Step 2. Join one A-C and one B-C unit as shown in Figure 4; repeat for four units. Join two units to complete a half center unit, again referring to Figure 4; repeat. Join the two units to complete an A-B-C unit; press seams in one direction.

Step 3. Sew D to every other C side of the pieced unit as shown in Figure 5; press seams toward D.

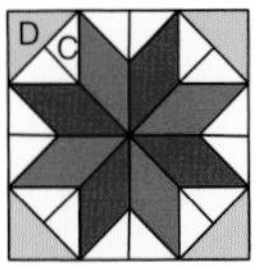

Figure 5
Sew D to every other C
side of the pieced unit.

Figure 6
Sew E to 2 adjacent
short sides of D.

Step 4. Sew E to two adjacent short sides of D as shown in Figure 6; repeat for four units. Press seams toward E.

Step 5. Sew a D-E unit to the remaining C sides of the pieced unit as shown in Figure 7; press seams toward D-E units.

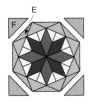

Figure 7
Sew a D-E unit to the
remaining C sides of
the pieced unit.

Figure 8
Add F to every other E
side of the pieced unit
to complete 1 block.

Step 6. Sew F to every other E side of the pieced unit to complete one block as shown in Figure 8; press seams toward F. Repeat for 20 blocks.

Completing the Top

Step 1. Arrange blocks in five rows of four blocks each referring to the Placement Diagram for positioning of blocks. Join blocks in rows; press seams in one direction.

Step 2. Join the rows to complete the pieced center; press seams in one direction.

Step 3. Sew a G strip to opposite long sides and H strips to the top and bottom of the pieced center; press seams toward G and H strips.

Finishing the Quilt

Step 1. Spray backing and top layers with basting spray as directed on product can. Sandwich the batting between the completed top and prepared backing; adjust as necessary to make flat.

Step 2. Hand- or machine-quilt as desired. When quilting is complete, trim batting and backing even with top.

Step 3. Join the binding strips on short ends to make one long strip. Fold the strip in half along length with wrong sides together; press.

Step 4. Sew binding to quilt edges, mitering corners and overlapping ends. Fold binding to the back side and stitch in place. ✱

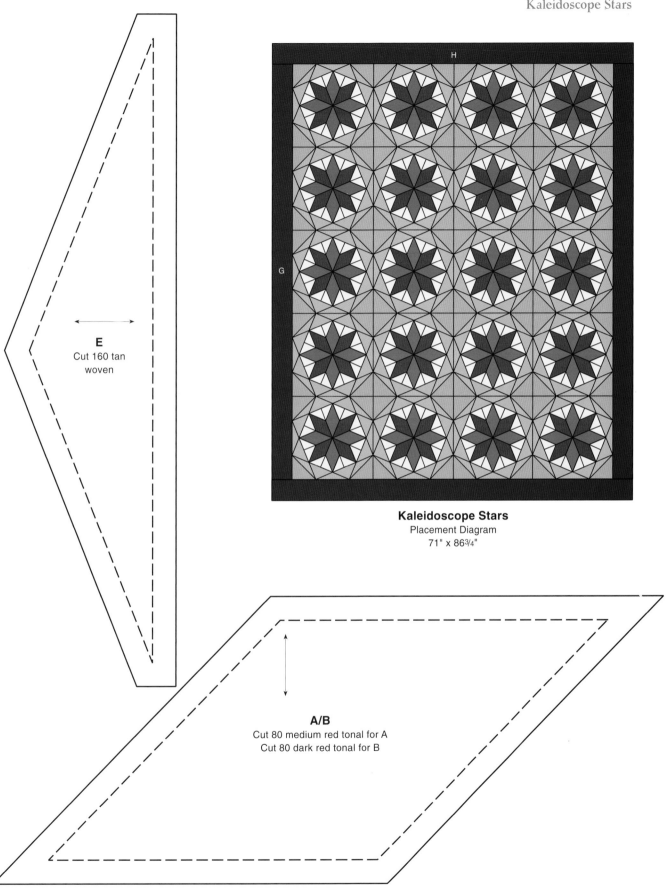

E
Cut 160 tan
woven

Kaleidoscope Stars
Placement Diagram
71" x 86¾"

A/B
Cut 80 medium red tonal for A
Cut 80 dark red tonal for B

DESIGN BY **TOBY LISCHKO**

Stairway to the Stars

Courthouse Steps blocks create stairs between the star blocks in this interlocking design.

Project Specifications

Skill Level: Intermediate
Quilt Size: 49" x 49"
Block Size: 7" x 7"
Number of Blocks: 29

Materials

- ¾ yard cream print
- 1¼ yards total red prints
- 1¼ yards total green prints
- 1¼ yards green bird print
- Backing 55" x 55"
- Batting 55" x 55"
- Neutral color all-purpose thread
- Quilting thread
- Basic sewing tools and supplies

Cutting

Step 1. Cut (10) 1½" by fabric width strips from green prints for Courthouse Steps blocks. Subcut strips into 24 segments in each of the following sizes: 3½" (#3), 5½" (#5) and 7½" (#7).

Step 2. Cut seven 1½" by fabric width strips from red prints for Courthouse Steps blocks. Subcut strips into 24 segments in each of the following sizes: 1½" (#2), 3½" (#4) and 5½" (#6).

Step 3. Cut one 1½" by fabric width strip cream print; subcut strip into (16) 1½" (#1) squares for Log Cabin and Courthouse Steps centers.

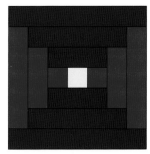

Courthouse Steps
7" x 7" Block

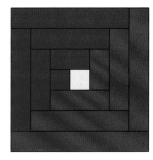

Log Cabin
7" x 7" Block

Green Star
7" x 7" Block

Red Star
7" x 7" Block

Step 4. Cut two 4" by fabric width strips cream print; subcut strips into (13) 4" A squares.

Step 5. Cut two strips green prints and four strips red prints 2¼" by fabric width; subcut strips into 2¼" B squares. You will need 32 green and 72 red B squares.

Step 6. Cut four 4¾" x 4¾" green print C squares and two 4¾" by fabric width strips red print; subcut strips into nine 4¾" red print C squares.

Step 7. Cut four 2⅝" by fabric width strips cream print; subcut strips into (52) 2⅝" D squares.

Step 8. Cut three 1½" by fabric width strips red prints; subcut strips into four each 1½" (#2), 2½" (#3), 3½" (#6), 4½" (#7), 5½" (#10) and 6½" (#11) for Log Cabin blocks.

Step 9. Cut three 1½" by fabric width strips green bird print; subcut strips into four each 2½" (#4), 3½" (#5), 4½" (#8), 5½" (#9), 6½" (#12) and 7½" (#13) for Log Cabin blocks.

Step 10. Cut three 1½" by fabric width strips red prints; subcut strips into 12 each 3½" E and 5½" G rectangles.

Step 11. Cut one 1½" by fabric width strip green print; subcut into (24) 1½" F squares.

Step 12. Cut three 2½" by fabric width strips green prints; subcut strips into (24) 1½" H rectangles and eight 7½" I strips.

Step 13. Cut four 5½" × 35½" J strips green bird print.

Step 14. Cut six 2¼" by fabric width strips green bird print for binding.

Making Courthouse Steps Blocks

Note: *The pieces for the Courthouse Steps and Log Cabin blocks have the same numbers but are different sizes. Refer to cutting instructions and figure drawings for block strips for correct numbered/sized pieces.*

Step 1. Referring to Figure 1, and beginning with piece 1, sew piece 2 to opposite sides of piece 1; press seams toward piece 2.

Figure 1
Sew piece 2 to opposite sides of piece 1.

Figure 2
Continue adding pieces in numerical order on opposite sides of the center to complete a Courthouse Steps block.

Step 2. Referring to Figure 2, continue adding pieces in numerical order on opposite sides of the center until all pieces are added; press all seams away from center to complete one Courthouse Steps block. Repeat for 12 blocks.

Making Star Blocks

Step 1. Draw a line from corner to corner on the wrong side of half the B squares and all of the D squares.

Step 2. Referring to Figure 3, place a B square right sides together on one corner of A; stitch on the marked line. Trim seam allowance to ¼"; press B to the right side.

 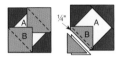

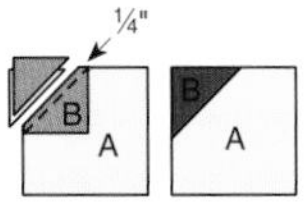

Figure 3
Place a B square right sides together on 1 corner of A; stitch on the marked line. Trim seam allowance to ¼"; press B to the right side.

Figure 4
Add B to all corners of A; stitch, trim and press to complete an A-B unit.

Step 3. Repeat Step 2 on each corner of A as shown in Figure 4 to complete an A-B unit; repeat for nine red A-B units and four green A-B units.

Step 4. Pin a D square on opposite corners of C with right sides together as shown in Figure 5; trim overlapping corners in the center as shown in Figure 6.

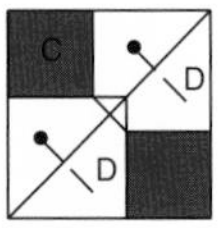

Figure 5
Pin a D square on opposite corners of C with right sides together.

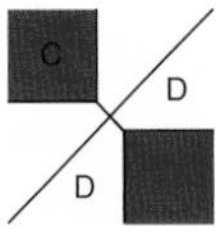

Figure 6
Trim overlapping corners in the center.

Step 5. Sew ¼" from each side of the marked lines through both D pieces as shown in Figure 7.

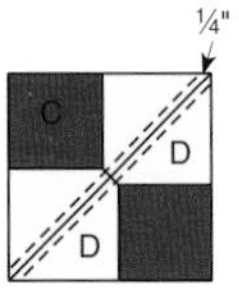

Figure 7
Sew ¼" from each side of the marked lines through both D pieces.

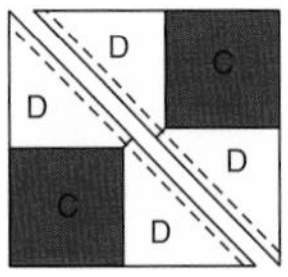

Figure 8
Cut along the marked lines to make 2 units.

Step 6. Cut along the marked lines to make two units as shown in Figure 8; press D pieces to the right side referring to Figure 9.

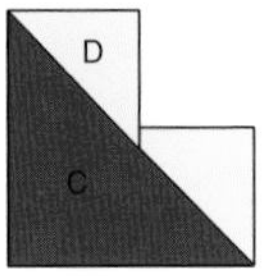

Figure 9
Press D pieces to the right side.

Step 7. Pin a D square to each unit as shown in Figure 10; stitch ¼" from the marked lines.

Figure 10
Pin a D square to each unit; stitch ¼" from the marked lines.

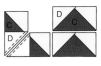

Figure 11
Cut units along marked line and press D to the right side to complete 2 C-D Flying Geese units.

Step 8. Referring to Figure 11, cut units along marked line and press D to the right side to complete two C-D Flying Geese units; repeat for 36 red and 16 green C-D units. *Note: If necessary, trim units to 2¼" x 4".*

Step 9. Sew a C-D unit to opposite sides of an A-B unit as shown in Figure 12; press seams toward the A-B unit.

Figure 12
Sew a C-D unit to opposite sides of an A-B unit.

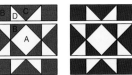

Figure 13
Join units to complete blocks as shown.

Step 10. Sew B to each end of a C-D unit; press seams toward B. Repeat for two units. Sew a B-C-D unit to opposite sides of the A-B-C-D unit to complete one block as shown in Figure 13; press seams away from block center. Repeat for nine Red and four Green Star blocks.

Making Corner Log Cabin Blocks

Step 1. Referring to Figure 14, sew pieces to the center #1 piece in numerical order, pressing seams away from the center; repeat for four blocks.

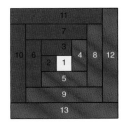

Figure 14
Sew pieces to center in numerical order as shown to make a Log Cabin block.

Completing the Top

Step 1. Join three Red Star blocks with two Courthouse Steps blocks to make a row as shown in Figure 15; press seams toward Courthouse Steps blocks. Repeat for three rows.

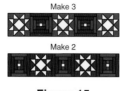

Figure 15
Join blocks to make rows.

Step 2. Join three Courthouse Steps blocks with two Green Star blocks to make a row, again referring to Figure 15; press seams toward Courthouse Steps blocks. Repeat for two rows.

Step 3. Join the rows referring to the Placement Diagram for positioning; press seams in one direction.

Step 4. Sew F to each end of E; repeat for 12 E-F units. Press seams toward F.

Step 5. Sew G to an E-F unit as shown in Figure 16; repeat for 12 units. Press seams toward G.

Figure 16
Sew G to an
E-F unit.

Figure 17
Sew H to each end
of each E-F-G unit.

Step 6. Sew H to each end of each E-F-G unit as shown in Figure 17; press seams toward H.

Step 7. Join three E-F-G-H units with two I strips to make a side unit as shown in Figure 18; repeat for four side units. Press seams toward I.

Figure 18
Join 3 E-F-G-H units with 2
I strips to make a side unit.

Step 8. Sew a J strip to each side unit as shown in Figure 19; press seams toward J.

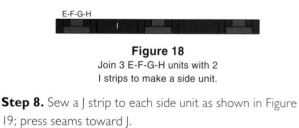

Figure 19
Sew a J strip to each side unit.

Step 9. Sew a J/side unit to opposite sides of the pieced center referring to the Placement Diagram for positioning; press seams toward J/side units.

Step 10. Sew a Log Cabin block to each end of each remaining J/side unit as shown in Figure 20; press seams toward blocks.

Figure 20
Sew a Log Cabin block to each end of
each remaining J/side unit.

Step 11. Sew the strips to the remaining sides of the pieced center to complete the top; press seams toward side strips.

Finishing the Quilt

Step 1. Sandwich the batting between the completed top and prepared backing; pin or baste layers together to hold.

Step 2. Hand- or machine-quilt as desired. When quilting is complete, trim batting and backing even with top; remove pins or basting.

Step 3. Join the binding strips on short ends to make one long strip. Fold the strip in half along length with wrong sides together; press.

Step 4. Sew binding to quilt edges, mitering corners and overlapping ends. Fold binding to the back side and stitch in place. ❄

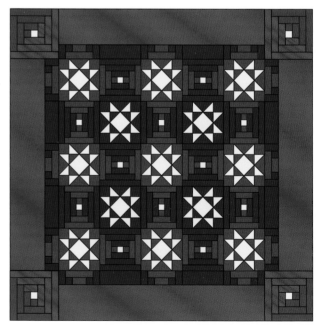

Stairway to the Stars
Placement Diagram
49" x 49"

Christmas Jewels

Create movement by changing the color of the corner triangles in the blocks of this pretty bed-size quilt.

Project Specifications

Skill Level: Beginner
Quilt Size: 80" x 92"
Block Size: 12" x 12"
Number of Blocks: 42

Materials

- 1 yard each pink and light green tonals
- 1⅛ yards red print
- 1¼ yards red tonal
- 2 yards green mottled
- 2½ yards cream tonal
- Backing 86" x 98"
- Batting 86" x 98"
- All-purpose thread to match fabrics
- Basic sewing tools and supplies

Cutting

Step 1. Cut eight 3½" by fabric width A strips cream tonal.
Step 2. Cut four 3½" by fabric width strips each red tonal (B) and green mottled (F).
Step 3. Cut (11) 5⅛" by fabric width strips cream tonal; subcut strips into (84) 5⅛" C squares. Cut each square on one diagonal to make 168 C triangles.
Step 4. Cut four 6⅞" by fabric width strips each pink (D), light green (G) and red (H) tonals and green mottled (E); subcut each color strip into (21) 6⅞" squares. Cut each square on one diagonal to make 42 triangles of each color.
Step 5. Cut eight 4½" by fabric width strips red print; join

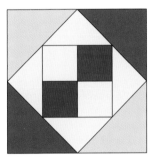 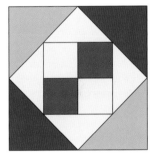

Pink Christmas Jewel
12" x 12" Block

Red Christmas Jewel
12" x 12" Block

strips on short ends to make one long strip. Subcut strip into two 84½" I strips and two 72½" J strips.
Step 6. Cut two 4½" x 4½" squares each pink (K) and light green (L) tonals.
Step 7. Cut nine 2¼" by fabric width strips green mottled for binding.

Making Blocks

Step 1. Sew an A strip to a B strip with right sides together along length; press seams toward B. Repeat for four strip sets.
Step 2. Subcut the A-B strip sets into (42) 3½" A-B segments as shown in Figure 1. Repeat with A and F strips to make 42 A-F segments.

Figure 1
Subcut strip sets
into 3½" segments.

Step 3. Join two A-B segments to make an A-B unit as shown in Figure 2; press seams in one direction. Repeat for 21 A-B units. Repeat with A-F segments to make 21 A-F units.

Figure 2
Join segments to
complete units.

Step 4. Sew C to each side of each A-B and A-F unit as shown in Figure 3; press seams toward C.

Figure 3
Sew C to each side
of the pieced units.

Step 5. Sew D to opposite corners of an A-B-C unit as shown in Figure 4; press seams toward D. Repeat with E on the remaining corners to complete one Pink Christmas Jewel block; press seams toward E. Repeat for 21 blocks.

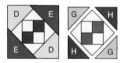

Figure 4
Sew triangles to opposite
corners of the pieced
center units.

Step 6. Repeat Step 5 with G and H triangles to complete 21 Red Christmas Jewel blocks, again referring to Figure 4.

Completing the Top

Step 1. Arrange blocks in seven rows of six blocks each referring to the Placement Diagram for positioning of blocks. Join blocks in rows; press seams toward red blocks.

Step 2. Join the rows to complete the pieced center; press seams in one direction.

Step 3. Sew an I strip to opposite long sides of the pieced center; press seams toward I.

Step 4. Sew a K square to one end and an L square to the other end of each J strip; press seams toward J.

Step 5. Sew a K-J-L strip to the top and bottom of the pieced center referring to the Placement Diagram for positioning; press seams toward the K-J-L strips.

Finishing the Quilt

Step 1. Sandwich the batting between the completed top and prepared backing; pin or baste layers together to hold.

Step 2. Hand- or machine-quilt as desired. When quilting is complete, trim batting and backing even with top; remove pins or basting.

Step 3. Join the binding strips on short ends to make one long strip. Fold the strip in half along length with wrong sides together; press.

Step 4. Sew binding to quilt edges, mitering corners and overlapping ends. Fold binding to the back side and stitch in place. ✳

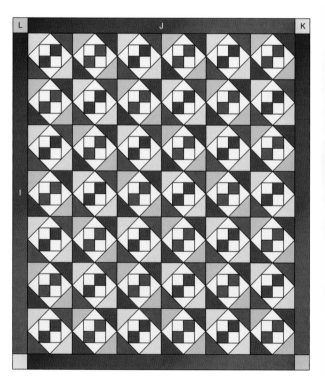

Christmas Jewels
Placement Diagram
80" x 92"

Starry Christmas Night

Although the Christmas Star dominated the night sky when Jesus was born, there were many other stars that night as well.

Project Specifications
Skill Level: Advanced
Quilt Size: 56" x 56"
Block Size: 12" x 12"
Number of Blocks: 16

Materials
- ½ yard dark blue solid
- ⅝ yard dark blue print
- ⅝ yard yellow mottled
- 1 yard dark blue tonal
- 1⅜ yards light blue solid
- 1¾ yards winter scenic print
- Backing 62" x 62"
- Batting 62" x 62"
- All-purpose thread to match fabrics
- Quilting thread
- 64 gold metallic star-shaped bangles
- 64 (3mm) gold beads
- Basic sewing tools and supplies

Cutting

Step 1. Prepare templates using pattern pieces given; cut as directed on each piece. **Note:** *The A pieces are cut diagonally from the winter scenic print to allow the motifs to be placed upright in the finished quilt. If your fabric is not directional, cut squares with edges along the straight fabric grain line.*

Step 2. Cut fabric pieces large enough to cover spaces on C paper-piecing pattern as follows: 128 each yellow mottled, dark blue print and light blue solid pieces.

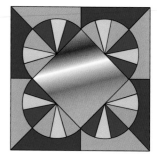

Starry Christmas Night
12" x 12" Block

Step 3. Cut two 4½" x 56½" E strips along the length of the winter scenic print; cut and piece two 4½" x 48½" D strips from the remaining width. **Note:** *The winter scenic print is directional, so side borders should be cut along length, while top and bottom borders should be cut across width. If your fabric is not directional, cut strips as desired to create sizes needed for borders.*

Step 4. Cut six 2¼" by fabric width strips dark blue solid for binding.

Completing the Blocks

Step 1. Make 128 copies of the C paper-piecing pattern.

Step 2. Lay a yellow mottled fabric piece right side up on the unmarked side of the paper-piecing pattern covering space 1 and extending at least ¼" beyond space all around.

Step 3. Pin a dark blue print piece right sides together with piece 1 as shown in Figure 1.

Figure 1
Pin a dark blue print piece right sides together with piece 1.

Step 4. Turn pattern over and stitch along the 1-2 line as shown in Figure 2.

 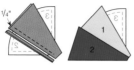

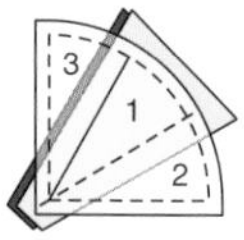

Figure 2
Turn over and stitch along 1-2 line as shown.

Figure 3
Flip and trim seam allowance to ¼" and finger-press piece 2 to the right side as shown.

Step 5. Turn over, trim seam allowance to ¼" and finger-press piece 2 to the right side as shown in Figure 3.
Step 6. Repeat Steps 3–5 for piece 3.
Step 7. Trim fabric even with pattern solid line to complete one dark blue C unit; repeat for 64 dark blue C units as shown in Figure 4. Repeat Steps 2–7 to complete 64 light blue C units, again referring to Figure 4.

Figure 4
Make 64 C units in each color combination as shown.

Figure 5
Sew B and BR to C units; join the B-C units as shown.

Step 8. Sew B to the light blue C units and BR to the dark blue C units as shown in Figure 5; press seams toward B and BR. Join one each B-C and BR-C unit, again referring to Figure 5; remove paper from C units.
Step 9. Sew a pieced unit to each side of A to complete one block referring to Figure 6; press seams toward A. Repeat for 16 blocks.

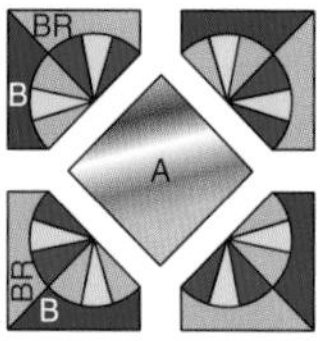

Figure 6
Sew the pieced units to A to complete 1 block.

Completing the Top
Step 1. Arrange blocks in four rows of four blocks each referring to Figure 7. Join blocks in rows; join rows to complete the pieced center; press seams in one direction.

Make 4

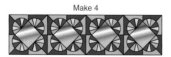

Figure 7
Arrange blocks in rows as shown.

Step 2. Sew D strips to the top and bottom and E strips to opposite sides of the pieced center; press seams toward strips.

Finishing the Quilt
Step 1. Sandwich the batting between the completed top and prepared backing; pin or baste layers together to hold.
Step 2. Hand- or machine-quilt as desired. When quilting is complete, trim batting and backing even with top; remove pins or basting.
Step 3. Join binding strips on short ends to make one long strip. Fold the strip in half along length with wrong sides together; press.
Step 4. Sew binding to quilt edges, mitering corners and overlapping ends. Fold binding to the back side and stitch in place.
Step 5. Sew star bangles and beads to quilt as shown in Figure 8. ✳

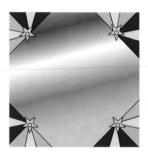

Figure 8
Sew star bangles and beads to quilt as shown.

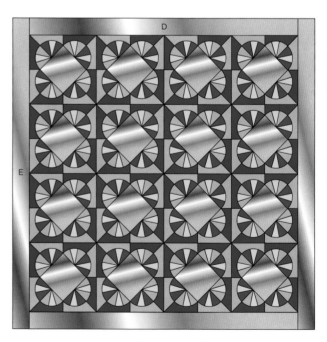

Starry Christmas Night
Placement Diagram
56" x 56"

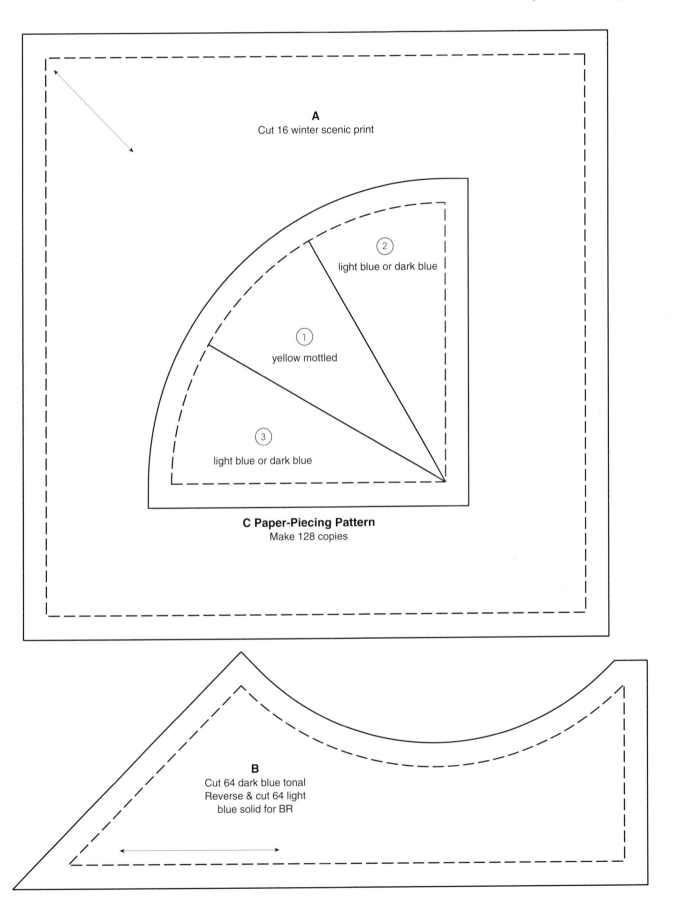

A
Cut 16 winter scenic print

②
light blue or dark blue

①
yellow mottled

③
light blue or dark blue

C Paper-Piecing Pattern
Make 128 copies

B
Cut 64 dark blue tonal
Reverse & cut 64 light
blue solid for BR

DESIGN BY **SANDRA L. HATCH**

Snowman Surprise

Use preprint squares or a large print as the center of the blocks in this holiday lap quilt.

Project Specifications
Skill Level: Beginner
Quilt Size: 48" x 63"
Block Size: 13" x 13"
Number of Blocks: 6

Materials
- 6 preprint squares or 6 squares large novelty print 7½" x 7½" (A)
- ¼ yard blue print 1
- ⅓ yard blue print 2
- ⅓ yard gold print
- ⅝ yard gold plaid
- 1¼ yards red tonal
- 1⅝ yards green tonal
- Backing 54" x 69"
- Batting 54" x 69"
- Neutral color all-purpose thread
- Quilting thread
- Basic sewing tools and supplies

Cutting
Step 1. Cut three 2" by fabric width strips gold plaid; subcut strips into six 7½" B and six 9" C strips.

Step 2. Cut three 2" by fabric width strips blue print 1; subcut strips into six 9" D and six 10½" E strips.

Step 3. Cut four 2" by fabric width strips gold print; subcut strips into six 10½" F strips and six 12" G strips.

Step 4. Cut four 2" by fabric width strips blue print 2; subcut strips into six 12" H strips and six 13½" I strips.

Snowman Log
13" x 13" Block

Step 5. Cut two 13½" by fabric width strips green tonal; subcut strips into (27) 3" J strips.

Step 6. Cut one 3" by fabric width strip red tonal; subcut strip into (12) 3" K squares.

Step 7. Cut two 3" by fabric width strips green tonal; subcut strips into (18) 3" L squares.

Step 8. Cut four 1¾" by fabric width strips red tonal; subcut strips into (96) 1¾" M squares. Draw a line from corner to corner on the wrong side of each square.

Step 9. Cut three 2¼" by fabric width strips gold plaid; join strips on short ends to make one long strip and press. Subcut strip into two 54½" N strips.

Step 10. Cut two 2½" x 42½" O strips gold plaid.

Step 11. Cut six 3½" by fabric width strips green tonal; subcut strips into (70) 3½" P squares.

Step 12. Cut seven 2" by fabric width strips red tonal; subcut strips into (132) 2" Q squares. Draw a line from corner to corner on the wrong side of each square.

Step 13. Cut six 2¼" by fabric width strips red tonal for binding.

Making Snowman Log Blocks

Step 1. Referring to Figure 1, sew B to A; press seams toward B.

Figure 1
Sew B to A.

Figure 2
Continue adding pieces around the center A square in alphabetical order to complete a block.

Step 2. Referring to Figure 2, continue adding pieces around the center A square in alphabetical order; press all seams away from center. Repeat for six Snowman Log blocks.

Completing the Top

Step 1. Referring to Figure 3, place an M square right sides together on one end of J; stitch on the marked line. Trim seam to ¼" and press M to the right side.

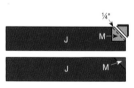

Figure 3
Place an M square right sides together on 1 end of J; stitch on the marked line. Trim seam to ¼" and press M to the right side.

Step 2. Repeat Step 1 on each corner of J referring to Figure 4 to complete a J-M unit. Repeat for 17 units.

Figure 4
Complete a J-M unit as shown.

Step 3. Join two blocks with three J-M units to make a row as shown in Figure 5; repeat for three rows. Press seams toward blocks.

Step 4. Join three K squares with two J-M units to make a sashing row as shown in Figure 6; repeat for four sashing rows. Press seams toward K.

Figure 5
Join 2 blocks with 3 J-M
units to make a row.

Figure 6
Join 3 K squares with 2 J-M
units to make a sashing row.

Step 5. Join the block rows with the sashing rows; press seams toward block rows.

Step 6. Sew M to two adjacent corners of L as in Step 1 and referring to Figure 7; repeat for 14 L-M units.

Step 7. Join two J strips and three L-M units as shown in Figure 8; repeat for two strips. Press seams toward J. Sew a strip to the top and bottom of the pieced center; press seams toward J-L-M strips.

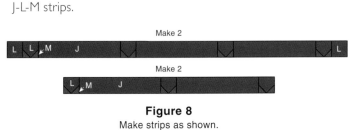

Make 2

Make 2

Figure 8
Make strips as shown.

Step 8. Join two L squares, three J strips and four L-M units to make a strip, again referring to Figure 8; repeat for two strips. Press seams toward J and L. Sew a strip to opposite sides of the pieced center; press seams toward J-L-M strips.

Step 9. Sew an N strip to opposite long sides and O strips to the top and bottom of the pieced center; press seams toward N and O.

Step 10. Complete 66 P-Q units as in Step 1 and referring to Figure 9.

Step 11. Join 19 P-Q units to make a side strip; repeat for two side strips. Press seams in one direction. Sew a side strip to opposite sides of the pieced center; press seams toward N strips.

Figure 7
Complete L-M
units as shown.

Figure 9
Complete a P-Q
unit as shown.

Step 12. Join 14 P-Q units with two P squares to make a strip; repeat for two strips. Press seams in one direction. Sew a strip to the top and bottom of the pieced center to complete the pieced top; press seams toward O strips.

Finishing the Quilt

Step 1. Sandwich the batting between the completed top and prepared backing; pin or baste layers together to hold.

Step 2. Hand- or machine-quilt as desired. When quilting is complete, trim batting and backing even with top; remove pins or basting.

Step 3. Join the binding strips on short ends to make one long strip. Fold the strip in half along length with wrong sides together; press.

Step 4. Sew binding to quilt edges, mitering corners and overlapping ends. Fold binding to the back side and stitch in place. ❄

Snowman Surprise
Placement Diagram
48" x 63"

Winter Snowfall

Make paper snowflake patterns of your own or use ours to make this sparkly table runner.

Project Specifications
Skill Level: Beginner
Runner Size: 36" x 21"

Materials
- 1 fat quarter each light and dark blue batiks
- ¼ yard white snowflake print
- ⅝ yard silver sparkle
- ⅝ yard blue snowflake print
- Backing 42" x 27"
- Batting 42" x 27"
- All-purpose thread to match fabrics
- Quilting thread
- ⅞ yard 18"-wide fusible web
- 5 (9") squares paper
- Basic sewing tools and supplies

Cutting
Step 1. Cut one 32½" x 17½" A rectangle from blue snowflake print.
Step 2. Cut seven 5¼" x 5¼" B squares white snowflake print; cut each square on both diagonals to make B triangles. You will need 26 B triangles.
Step 3. Cut two light blue batik and five dark blue batik 5¼" x 5¼" squares. Cut each square on both diagonals to make C triangles; you will need seven light blue and 19 dark blue C triangles.
Step 4. Prepare template for D; cut as directed on the piece.

Step 5. Cut four 2¼" by fabric width strips silver sparkle for binding.

Making Snowflake Shapes
Step 1. Fold each paper square as shown in Figure 1.

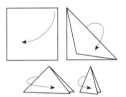

Figure 1
Fold each paper square.

Figure 2
Trace a snowflake
onto 1 side of a
folded paper triangle.

Step 2. Trace a snowflake design given onto one side of each folded paper triangle as shown in Figure 2.
Note: You may make your own snowflake designs or use those provided.
Step 3. Cut out paper snowflake shapes along drawn lines through all layers.
Step 4. Unfold paper patterns; iron flat.
Step 5. Lay each pattern on the paper side of the fusible web; trace. Cut out shapes ⅛"–¼" from outside drawn lines.
Step 6. Fuse pattern shapes to the wrong side of silver sparkle; cut on marked lines. **Note:** *You will need very sharp, pointed scissors to cut inside small areas.*
Step 7. Remove paper backing.

Completing the Runner Top

Step 1. Arrange the fabric snowflake shapes on the A background referring to the Placement Diagram for positioning; fuse shapes in place.

Step 2. Join nine B and three light and five dark blue C triangles to make a side strip as shown in Figure 3; press seams toward C. Repeat with nine B and two light and six dark blue C triangles.

Figure 3
Join 9 B and 8 C triangles
to make a side strip.

Step 3. Sew B to each side of a light blue C and add D and DR as shown in Figure 4; press seams toward C. Add one B and two dark blue C triangles to each side of each pieced unit to complete an end strip as shown in Figure 5; press seams toward C. Repeat for two end strips.

Figure 4
Sew B to each side of
C and add D and DR.

Figure 5
Add 1 B and 2 C
triangles to each side
of each pieced unit to
complete an end strip.

Step 4. Sew an end strip to opposite ends of A, stopping stitching ¼" from ends of A as shown in Figure 6.

Figure 6
Sew an end strip to
opposite ends of A,
stopping stitching ¼"
from ends of A.

Figure 7
Fold quilt at corners
and complete seam
joining corner B and
C triangles.

Step 5. Sew a side strip to opposite sides of A, stopping stitching ¼" from ends of A.

Step 6. Fold quilt at corners and complete seam joining corner B and C triangles, starting at the end of the

Winter Snowfall
Placement Diagram
36" x 21"

previously stitched strip seams as shown in Figure 7; press seams toward pieced strips.

Finishing the Runner

Step 1. Sandwich the batting between the completed top and prepared backing; pin or baste layers together to hold.

Step 2. Hand- or machine-quilt as desired. When quilting is complete, trim batting and backing even with top; remove pins or basting.

Step 3. Join the binding strips on short ends to make one long strip. Fold the strip in half along length with wrong sides together; press.

Step 4. Sew binding to quilt edges, mitering corners and overlapping ends. Fold binding to the back side and stitch in place. ✳

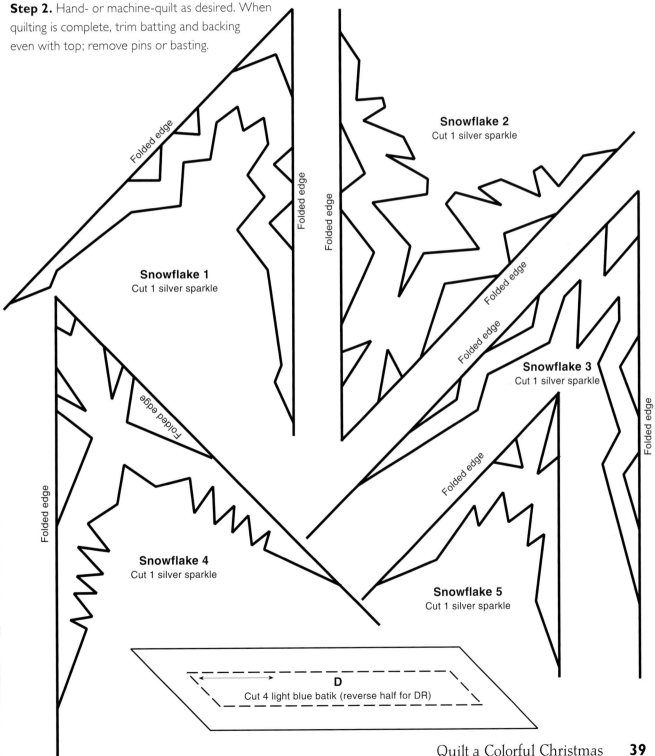

Visions of Snowmen

Appliquéd tree and snowman blocks with 3-D elements are sure to be popular with youngsters during the winter holiday season.

Project Specifications

Skill Level: Intermediate
Quilt Size: 67½" x 90"
Block Size: 7½" x 10"
Number of Blocks: 30

Materials

- ⅛ yard each black and brown prints
- ½ yard yellow tonal
- ⅔ yard each red plaid and green-and-white stripe
- 2 yards green print
- 2 yards blue print
- 2⅛ yards red print
- 2¼ yards white/gold print
- Backing 74" x 96"
- Batting 74" x 96"
- All-purpose thread to match fabrics
- ⅓ yard 18"-wide fusible web
- Basic sewing tools and supplies

Cutting

Step 1. Cut three 10½" by fabric width strips each white/gold (A) and blue (B) prints; subcut strips into (15) 8" A and B rectangles.

Step 2. Cut four 3" by fabric width E strips each blue print, green print, red print, green-and-white stripe, red plaid and yellow tonal.

Step 3. Cut (17) 3" by fabric width strips red print; subcut six strips into (30) 8" C rectangles. Join the remaining strips on short ends to make one long strip; subcut strip into six 75½" D strips.

Tree
7½" x 10" Block

Snowman
7½" x 10" Block

Step 4. Prepare templates for appliqué shapes using patterns given; fold the white/gold print, green-and-white stripe, red plaid and green print fabrics in half along length with right sides together; pin layers to secure. Trace snowman, bow and tree shapes as directed on each piece onto the double layers, leaving ½" between shapes. Add pins to each traced shape to hold layers together.

Step 5. Cut two 3" x 9", one 7" x 9" and one 4" x 9" rectangle fusible web. Bond the 3" x 9" rectangles to the wrong side of the red print and yellow tonal, the 7" x 9" rectangle to the black print and the 4" x 9" rectangle to the brown print.

Step 6. Trace the button, ornament and trunk shapes onto the paper side of the fused fabrics as directed on patterns for color and number to cut; cut out shapes on traced lines. Remove paper backing.

Step 7. Cut two 8" x 8" squares each red (F) and green (G) prints.

Step 8. Cut nine 2¼" by fabric width strips blue print for binding.

Completing Appliquéd Blocks

Step 1. With traced snowman shapes still pinned with right sides together, stitch around each layered shape on the marked lines. When all shapes have been stitched, cut out each shape, leaving a seam allowance around each one as shown in Figure 1.

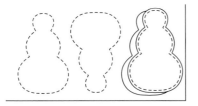

Figure 1
Cut out shapes, leaving a seam
allowance around each.

Step 2. Clip curves and cut to inner corners as shown in Figure 2.

Figure 2
Clip curves and cut
to inner corners.

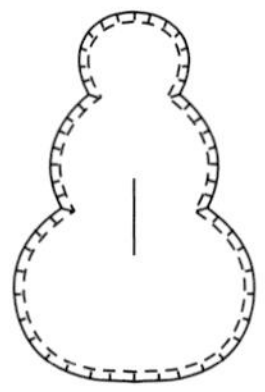

Figure 3
Cut a small slit in the center
of 1 side of a stitched motif.

Step 3. Cut a small slit in the center of one side of each motif as shown in Figure 3; turn right side out through cut opening. Smooth curved edges; press flat.

Step 4. Repeat Steps 1–3 to complete bows and trees.

Step 5. Center and fuse three buttons to each snowman referring to the pattern for placement; repeat with ornaments on trees, placing three yellow on seven trees and three red on eight trees.

Step 6. Machine-stitch around button and ornament shapes using a narrow zigzag stitch and matching thread.

Step 7. Center a snowman shape on a B rectangle; hand-stitch in place ½" from edge using matching thread.

Step 8. Pin a bow to each stitched snowman; stitch at side edges of snowman and across top and bottom center edges to secure as shown in Figure 4. **Note:** *The bow ends are left unstitched.* Repeat Steps 7 and 8 to complete 15 Snowman blocks.

Figure 4
Stitch bow to
snowman.

Step 9. Arrange a tree and trunk shape on an A rectangle; fuse trunk shape in place. Hand-stitch tree shape in place as for snowman and stitch trunk in place as for snowman buttons. Repeat for 15 blocks.

Completing the Top

Step 1. Join three Tree blocks with three Snowman blocks and six C strips as shown in Figure 5 to make a row; repeat for five rows. Press seams toward C strips.

Figure 5
Join blocks with C to make rows.

Step 2. Arrange the rows referring to the Placement Diagram. Join the rows with D strips to complete the pieced center; press seams toward D.

Step 3. Join one E strip of each color with right sides together along length in the color order shown in Figure 6; press seams in one direction. Repeat for four strip sets. Subcut strip sets into (17) 8" E units, again referring to Figure 6.

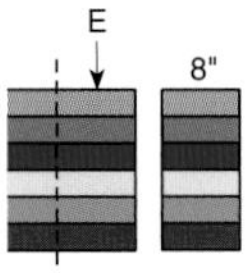

Figure 6
Join 1 E strip of each
color with right sides
together along length
in the color order
shown; subcut strip
sets into 8" E units.

Step 4. Join five units as shown in Figure 7 to make the right side border strip. Press seams in one direction. Sew to the right side of the pieced center; press seam toward D.

Figure 7
Join 5 units to make a side border strip.

Step 5. Join six E units as shown in Figure 8; remove a blue print, red plaid and green print section from one end and a yellow tonal, green-and-white stripe and red print section from the opposite end to make left side border strip, again referring to Figure 8.

Figure 8
Join 6 E units; remove a 3-segment section from each end.

Step 6. Sew the strip to the left side of the pieced center; press seam toward D.

Step 7. Join three E units as shown in Figure 9; repeat for two strips. Add the blue-red-green three-segment section to the red print end of one strip and the yellow-green-red three-segment section to the blue print end of the second strip, again referring to Figure 9.

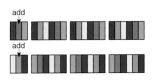

Figure 9
Join 3 E units; sew the 3-segment removed sections to 1 end of each strip.

Step 8. Sew an F square to one end and a G square to the opposite end of each E strip to complete the top and bottom border strips as shown in Figure 10; press seams toward squares.

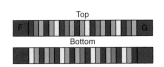

Figure 10
Add G and F squares to the top and bottom border strips.

Step 9. Sew the strips to the top and bottom of the pieced center to complete the top referring to the Placement Diagram for positioning of strips; press seams toward strips.

Finishing the Quilt

Step 1. Sandwich the batting between the completed top and prepared backing; pin or baste layers together to hold.

Step 2. Hand- or machine-quilt as desired. When quilting is complete, trim batting and backing even with top; remove pins or basting.

Step 3. Join the binding strips on short ends to make one long strip. Fold the strip in half along length with wrong sides together; press.

Step 4. Sew binding to quilt edges, mitering corners and overlapping ends. Fold binding to the back side and stitch in place. ❄

Visions of Snowmen
Placement Diagram
67½" x 90"

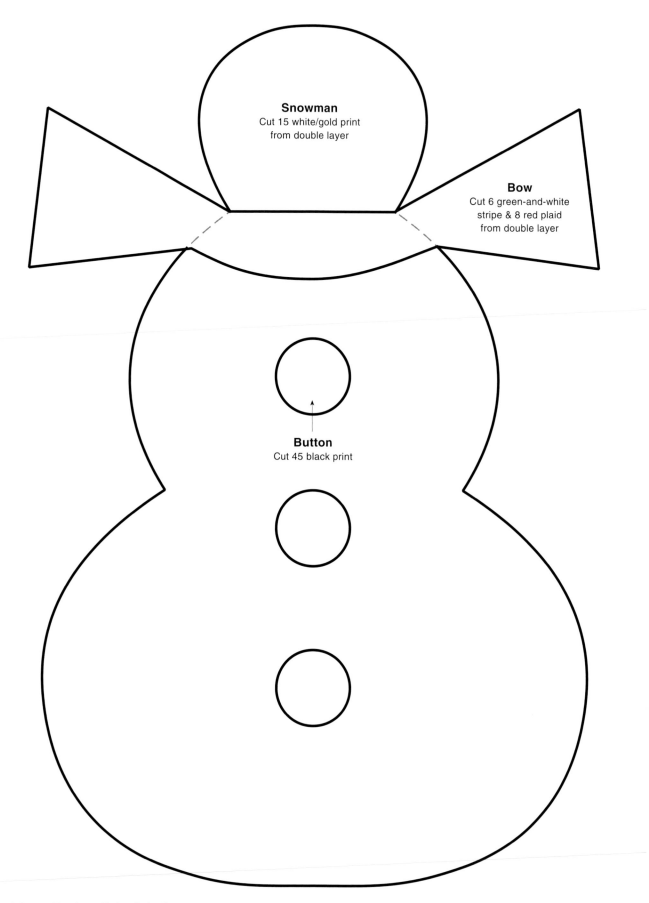

Snowman
Cut 15 white/gold print
from double layer

Bow
Cut 6 green-and-white
stripe & 8 red plaid
from double layer

Button
Cut 45 black print

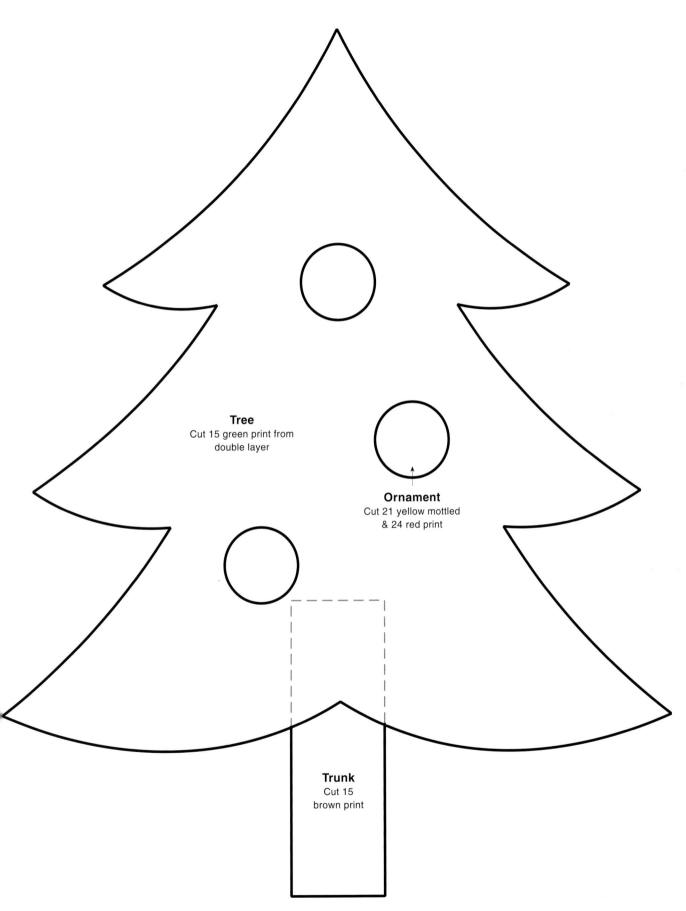

Tree
Cut 15 green print from
double layer

Ornament
Cut 21 yellow mottled
& 24 red print

Trunk
Cut 15
brown print

DESIGN BY **KARLA SCHULZ**

Homespun Christmas

Three different pieced blocks combine in this large Christmas wall quilt.

Project Specifications

Skill Level: Intermediate
Quilt Size: 58" x 58"
Block Size: 10" x 10"
Number of Blocks: 9

Materials

- 1 yard tan speckled
- 1 yard cream check
- 1⅝ yards green plaid
- 1⅝ yards red dot
- Backing 64" x 64"
- Batting 64" x 64"
- Neutral color all-purpose thread
- Quilting thread
- Basic sewing tools and supplies

Cutting

Step 1. Cut one 10½" by fabric width strip cream check; subcut into four 10½" A squares.

Step 2. Cut three 5½" by fabric width strips red dot; subcut strips into (16) 5½" B squares; mark a line from corner to corner on the wrong side of each square.

Step 3. Cut six 2½" by fabric width strips tan speckled; subcut one strip into eight 2½" H squares. Set aside remaining strips for C and P.

Step 4. Cut eight 2½" by fabric width strips red dot for D and O.

Step 5. Cut two 4½" by fabric width strips cream check; subcut seven 2½" E rectangles from one strip. Set aside remainder of strip and the remaining strip for D-E units.

Christmas Tree
10" x 10" Block

Square-in-a-Square
10" x 10" Block

Sashed Four-Patch
10" x 10" Block

Step 6. Cut two 2⅞" by fabric width strips each tan speckled (F) and green plaid (G); subcut each color strip into (28) 2⅞" squares. Cut each square in half on one diagonal to make 56 each F and G triangles.

Step 7. Cut one 6⅞" by fabric width strip green plaid; subcut into two 6⅞" I squares and four 2¼" x 5½" K rectangles. Cut each I square in half on one diagonal to make four I triangles.

Step 8. Cut two 6" x 6" squares tan speckled; cut each square on both diagonals to make eight J triangles.

Step 9. Cut one 2½" by fabric width L strip green plaid.

Step 10. Cut eight 4½" by fabric width strips green plaid for M and Q borders.

Step 11. Cut one 8½" by fabric width strip cream check; subcut into (16) 2½" N rectangles.

Step 12. Cut six 2¼" by fabric width strips red dot for binding.

Making Square-in-a-Square Blocks

Step 1. Place a B square on one corner of A and stitch on the marked line as shown in Figure 1; trim seam to ¼" and press B to the right side.

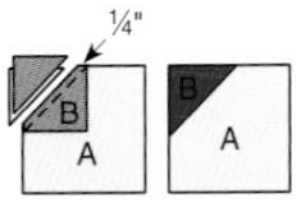

Figure 1
Place a B square on 1 corner
of A and stitch on the marked
line; trim seam to ¼" and press
B to the right side.

Step 2. Repeat Step 1 on the remaining corners of A as shown in Figure 2 to complete one Square-in-a-Square block; repeat for four blocks.

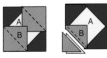

Figure 2
Sew B to each
corner of A.

Making Sashed Four-Patch Blocks

Step 1. Sew a C strip to a D strip and a P strip to an O strip with right sides together along length; press seams toward D and O. Repeat for five strip sets; subcut into (48) 2½" C-D units and (16) 4½" O-P units as shown in Figure 3. Set aside 32 C-D units and all O-P units for borders.

Figure 3
Subcut strip sets into
2½" C-D units and
4½" O-P units.

Step 2. Join two C-D units as shown in Figure 4 to make

a Four-Patch unit; repeat for eight units. Press seams in one direction. Set aside four Four-Patch units for borders.

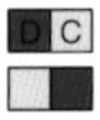

Figure 4
Join 2 C-D units to
make a Four-Patch unit.

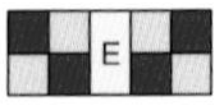

Figure 5
Join 2 Four-Patch
units with E.

Step 3. Join two Four-Patch units with an E rectangle as shown in Figure 5; repeat for two C-D-E rows. Press seams toward E.

Step 4. Sew a D strip to an E strip with right sides together along length; repeat for a partial D-E strip using uncut remainder of E strip. Press seams toward D.

Step 5. Subcut strip sets into (17) 2½" D-E units as shown in Figure 6; set aside 16 units for borders.

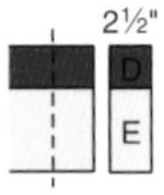

Figure 6
Subcut strip sets
into 2½" D-E units

Figure 7
Sew E to a
D-E unit.

Step 6. Sew E to a D-E unit as shown in Figure 7; press seams toward D.

Step 7. Join the C-D-E rows with the E-D-E unit as shown in Figure 8 to complete the Sashed Four-Patch block.

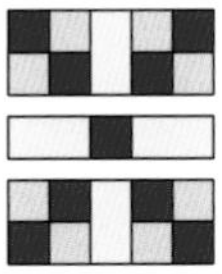

Figure 8
Join units to
complete the block.

Making Christmas Tree Blocks

Step 1. Sew F to G to make an F-G unit as shown in Figure 9; repeat for 56 units. Press seams toward G.

Figure 9
Sew F to G to
make an F-G unit.

Figure 10
Join 2 J
triangles with K.

Step 2. Join two J triangles with K as shown in Figure 10; press seams toward K.

Step 3. Trim K to make a square corner as shown in Figure 11. Repeat for four J-K units.

Figure 11
Trim K to make a
square corner.

Figure 12
Sew I to a J-K unit.

Step 4. Sew I to a J-K unit as shown in Figure 12; press seams toward I. Repeat for four units.

Step 5. Join four F-G units to make a row as shown in Figure 13; repeat with three F-G units, again referring to Figure 13. Press seams in one direction. Repeat for eight each four- and three-unit rows.

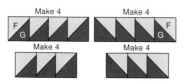

Figure 13
Make 3-unit and 4-unit F-G rows.

Step 6. To complete one Christmas Tree block, sew a three-unit F-G row to an I-J-K unit as shown in Figure 14; press seams toward I.

Step 7. Sew H to the G end of a three-unit F-G row and sew to the pieced unit, again referring to Figure 14.

Figure 14
Sew H to the G end of
a 3-unit F-G row; sew
to the pieced unit.

Figure 15
Join units to
complete 1 block.

Step 8. Sew a four-unit F-G row to the pieced unit as shown in Figure 15; press seams in one direction.

Step 9. Sew H to the G end of a four-unit F-G row and sew to the pieced unit, again referring to Figure 15 to complete one block; press seams in one direction. Repeat for four blocks.

Completing the Top

Step 1. Referring to the Placement Diagram for positioning of blocks, join two Christmas Tree blocks with one

Square-in-a-Square block to make a row; repeat for two rows. Press seams toward center block.

Step 2. Join two Square-in-a-Square blocks with the Sashed Four-Patch block to make the center row; press seams away from center block.

Step 3. Join the rows to complete the pieced center; press seams toward center row.

Step 4. Sew an L strip to a D strip with right sides together along length; press seams toward L.

Step 5. Subcut strip set into (16) 2½" D-L units as shown in Figure 16.

Figure 16
Subcut strip set into
2½" D-L units.

Figure 17
Join units to complete
a D-L Four-Patch unit.

Step 6. Join two D-L units to make a D-L Four-Patch unit as shown in Figure 17; repeat for eight units.

Step 7. Join the M/Q strips on short ends to make one long strip; press. Subcut strip into four 30½" M strips and four 50½" Q strips.

Step 8. Sew an M strip to opposite sides of the pieced center; press seams toward M.

Step 9. Sew a D-L Four-Patch unit to each end of the remaining M strips referring to the Placement Diagram for positioning; press seams toward M.

Step 10. Sew a D-L-M strip to the remaining sides of the pieced center, again referring to the Placement Diagram for positioning of strips; press seams toward strips.

Step 11. Referring to Figure 18, sew two C-D units to an O-P unit; press seams in one direction. Add N to complete a side unit; press seams toward N. Repeat for 16 side units.

Figure 18
Sew 2 C-D units to an O-P unit; add N to complete a side unit.

Step 12. Join four side units with three D-E units to make a side row as shown in Figure 19; repeat for four side rows.

Figure 19
Join 4 side units with 3 D-E units to make a side row.

Step 13. Sew a side row to opposite sides of the pieced center; press seams away from side rows.

Step 14. Sew E to a C-D Four-Patch unit; add a D-E unit to complete a corner unit as shown in Figure 20; repeat for four corner units. Press seams toward E and D-E.

Figure 20
Sew E to a C-D Four-Patch unit; add a D-E unit to complete a corner unit.

Step 15. Sew a corner unit to each end of the remaining side rows as shown in Figure 21; press seams toward corner units.

Figure 21
Sew a corner unit to each end of the remaining side rows.

Step 16. Sew the pieced side/corner units to the remaining sides of the pieced center.

Step 17. Sew a Q strip to opposite sides of the pieced center; press seams toward Q.

Step 18. Sew a D-L Four-Patch unit to each end of the remaining Q strips referring to the Placement Diagram for positioning.

Step 19. Sew the strips to opposite sides of the pieced center to complete the top referring to the Placement Diagram for positioning of strips.

Finishing the Quilt

Step 1. Sandwich the batting between the completed top and prepared backing; pin or baste layers together to hold.

Step 2. Hand- or machine-quilt as desired. When quilting is complete, trim batting and backing even with top; remove pins or basting.

Step 3. Join the binding strips on short ends to make one long strip. Fold the strip in half along length with wrong sides together; press.

Step 4. Sew binding to quilt edges, mitering corners and overlapping ends. Fold binding to the back side and stitch in place. ✳

Homespun Christmas
Placement Diagram
58" x 58"

DESIGN BY **LUCY A. FAZELY & MICHAEL L. BURNS**

Connecting Wreaths

Small Nine-Patches form wreaths on this bed-size holiday quilt.

Project Specifications
Skill Level: Beginner
Quilt Size: 72" x 87"
Block Size: 15" x 15"
Number of Blocks: 20

Materials
- ½ yard tan mottled
- ½ yard pale yellow print
- ½ yard burgundy tonal
- ¾ yard gold tonal
- 1 yard dark green tonal
- 2⅛ yards cream tonal
- 3⅛ yards medium green print
- Backing 78" x 93"
- Batting 78" x 93"
- Neutral color all-purpose thread
- Quilting thread
- Basting spray
- Basic sewing tools and supplies

Cutting

Step 1. Cut the following fabric-width strips from cream tonal: (24) 1½" A and nine 3½"—subcut into (100) 3½" B squares.

Step 2. Cut four 3½" by fabric width strips each tan mottled (C) and pale yellow print (D); subcut strips into 40 each 3½" C and D squares.

Step 3. Cut (14) 1½" by fabric width E strips gold tonal.

Step 4. Cut nine 1½" by fabric width F strips burgundy tonal.

Step 5. Cut (33) 1½" by fabric width G strips medium green print.

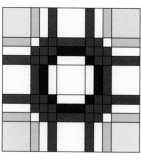

Connecting Wreath
15" x 15" Block

Step 6. Cut (10) 1½" by fabric width H strips dark green tonal.

Step 7. Cut seven 2½" by fabric width strips dark green tonal; join strips on short ends to make one long strip. Subcut strips into two 75½" I and two 64½" J strips.

Step 8. Cut eight 4½" by fabric width strips medium green print; join strips on short ends to make one long strip. Subcut strips into two 79½" K and two 72½" L strips.

Step 9. Cut eight 2¼" by fabric width strips medium green print for binding.

Piecing the Blocks

Step 1. Referring to Figure 1, join one each G, A and E strips with right sides together along length; press seams in one direction. Repeat for 14 G-A-E strip sets; subcut strip sets into (160) 3½" G-A-E units.

Step 2. Referring to Figure 1, repeat Step 1 to make seven A-H-G strip sets; subcut into (80) 3½" A-H-G units.

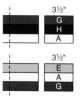

Figure 1
Join strips and
subcut as shown.

Step 3. Referring to Figure 2, join strips with right sides together along length to make three each F-G-A, G-F-G and H-G-F strip sets; subcut each strip set into 1½" segments to make 80 each F-G-A, G-F-G and H-G-F units.

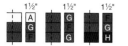

Figure 2
Join strips and subcut as shown.

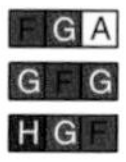

Figure 3
Make a Nine-Patch
unit as shown.

Step 4. Join one each F-G-A, G-F-G and H-G-F unit to complete a Nine-Patch unit as shown in Figure 3; press seams in one direction.

Step 5. To piece one block, join C with a G-A-E unit with B with a G-A-E unit and D to make a row referring to Figure 4; repeat for two rows. Press seams toward B, C and D.

Figure 4
Join C with a G-A-E unit with B with a
G-A-E unit and D to make a row.

Step 6. Join a G-A-E unit with a Nine-Patch unit with an A-H-G unit with a Nine-Patch unit with a G-A-E unit to make a row referring to Figure 5; repeat for two rows. Press seams toward Nine-Patch units.

Figure 5
Join a G-A-E unit with a Nine-Patch unit
with an A-H-G unit with a Nine-Patch unit
with a G-A-E unit to make a row.

Step 7. Join three B squares with two A-H-G units to make a row referring to Figure 6; press seams toward B.

Step 8. Join the rows as shown in Figure 7 to complete one block; press seams in one direction. Repeat for 20 blocks.

Figure 6
Join 3 B squares with 2 A-H-G
units to make a row.

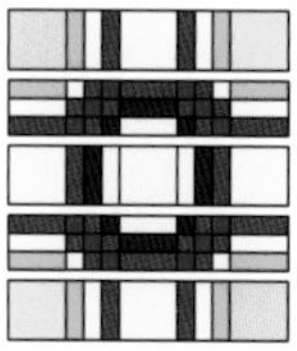

Figure 7
Join the rows as shown
to complete 1 block.

Completing the Top

Step 1. Join four blocks to make a row; press seams in one direction. Repeat for five rows.

Step 2. Join the rows with seams in adjoining rows going in opposite directions to complete the pieced center; press seams in one direction.

Step 3. Sew an I strip to opposite long sides and J strips to the top and bottom of the pieced center; press seams toward strips.

Step 4. Sew a K strip to opposite long sides and L strips to the top and bottom of the pieced center; press seams toward strips.

Finishing the Quilt

Step 1. Spray backing and top layers with basting spray as directed on product can. Sandwich the batting between the completed top and prepared backing; adjust as necessary to make flat.

Step 2. Hand- or machine-quilt as desired. When quilting is complete, trim batting and backing even with top.

Step 3. Join the binding strips on short ends to make one long strip. Fold the strip in half along length with wrong sides together; press.

Step 4. Sew binding to quilt edges, mitering corners and overlapping ends. Fold binding to the back side and stitch in place. ❊

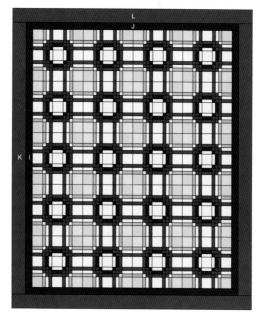

Connecting Wreaths
Placement Diagram
72" x 87"

DESIGN BY **SANDRA L. HATCH**

Christmas Swirls

A holiday stripe keeps the pieces swirling in this holiday quilt.

Project Specifications

Skill Level: Intermediate
Quilt Size: 62" x 62"
Block Size: 12" x 12"
Number of Blocks: 16

Materials

- ¾ yard gold print
- 1⅛ yards cream/green dot
- 1⅛ yards green/red dot
- 1⅛ yards red/cream dot
- 1¾ yards red stripe
- Backing 68" x 68"
- Batting 68" x 68"
- All-purpose thread to match fabrics
- Quilting thread
- Basic sewing tools and supplies

Cutting

Step 1. Cut two 6⅞" by fabric width strips each cream/green dot (A) and gold print (B); subcut A and B strips into eight 6⅞" squares each. Cut each square in half on one diagonal to make 16 triangles each.

Step 2. Cut two 6½" by fabric width strips each cream/green dot (C and CR) and red/cream dot (D and DR). Subcut strips into (16) 4⅛" rectangles each fabric. Prepare template for C/D using pattern given. Lay the template on the rectangles as shown in Figure 1 to cut 16 each C and CR cream/green dot and 16 each D and DR red/cream dot.

Figure 1
Cut C, CR, D and DR pieces as shown.

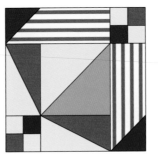

Christmas Swirls 1
12" x 12" Block

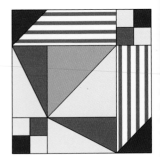

Christmas Swirls 2
12" x 12" Block

Step 3. Cut three 9½" by fabric width strips red stripe; subcut strips into (32) 3½" E rectangles.

Step 4. Cut three 3½" by fabric width strips green/red dot; subcut strips into (32) 3½" F squares. Mark a line from corner to corner on the wrong side of each square.

Step 5. Cut two strips each red/cream (H) and green/red (I) dots and four strips cream/green dot (G) 2" by fabric width.

Step 6. Cut five 1½" by fabric width strips gold print; join strips on short ends to make one long strip. Subcut strip into two 48½" J strips and two 50½" K strips.

Step 7. Cut five 2½" by fabric width strips green/red dot; join strips on short ends to make one long strip. Subcut strip into two 50½" L strips and two 54½" M strips.

Step 8. Cut six 4½" by fabric width strips red stripe; join strips on short ends to make one long strip. **Note:** *If you join the stripe strips carefully, you should not be able to see the seam or an interruption in the stripe design.* Subcut strip into four 54½" N strips.

Step 9. Cut four 4½" x 4½" O squares green/red dot.

Quilty Santa

Embroidered snowflakes create a puffy design in the background of this redwork Santa.

Project Specifications
Skill Level: Beginner
Quilt Size: 18" x 23"

Materials
- 13½" x 18½" rectangle white solid for A
- ½ yard red print
- Backing 22" x 27"
- Batting 22" x 27"
- All-purpose thread to match fabrics
- White 6-strand embroidery floss
- Variegated red No. 12 pearl cotton
- Basic sewing tools and supplies and embroidery hoop

Cutting
Step 1. Cut four 3" x 18½" B strips red print.
Step 2. Cut three 2¼" by fabric width strips red print for binding.

Embroidered Center
Step 1. Fold the A rectangle and crease to mark the center.
Step 2. Transfer the Santa design to A, matching center mark on design with creased center of A.
Step 3. Using the No. 12 variegated red pearl cotton, stem-stitch all straight lines on the design. Make French knots for small circles. Fill in button circles with lots of French knots. Make snowflakes with straight stitches as shown in Figure 1.

Figure 1
Stitch
snowflake
as shown.

Finishing the Quilt
Step 1. Sew a B strip to opposite long sides and to the top and bottom of the embroidered center; press seams toward B strips.
Step 2. Sandwich batting between the completed top and prepared backing piece; baste layers together to hold flat.
Step 3. Using an embroidery hoop and a needle threaded with 2 strands of white embroidery floss, randomly stitch snowflakes about ¾" apart over the entire A background and on Santa, referring to Figure 1.
Step 4. When finished with embroidery, quilt remainder of wall quilt as desired by hand or machine.
Step 5. Join the binding strips on short ends to make one long strip. Fold the strip in half along length with wrong sides together; press.
Step 6. Sew binding to quilt edges, mitering corners and overlapping ends. Fold binding to the back side and stitch in place. ✳

Quilty Santa
Placement Diagram
18" x 23"

Match on line to make complete pattern.

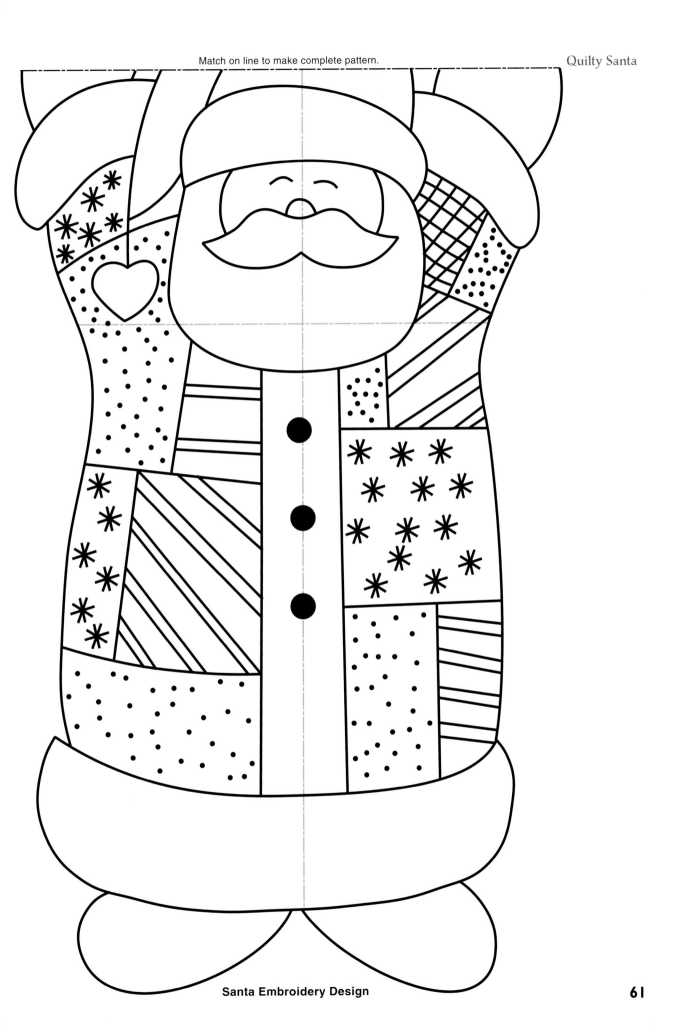

Santa Embroidery Design

Holly & Ivy Flannel Throw

Plain strips, simple squares and subdued colors accented by appliquéd shapes give this oversized throw a somewhat masculine look that is perfect for a man's study or den at holiday time.

Project Specifications

Skill Level: Beginner
Quilt Size: 64" x 64"

Materials

Note: *All fabrics listed are flannel.*

- ⅓ yard red solid
- ⅜ yard medium green mottled
- ½ yard cream tonal
- ½ yard cream print
- ½ yard dark green print
- ¾ yard moss green mottled
- 1¼ yards burgundy mottled
- 1⅜ yards gray print
- 1⅜ yards black print
- Backing 70" x 70"
- Batting 70" x 70"
- All-purpose thread to match fabrics
- Quilting thread
- Heat-resistant template material
- Spray sizing
- Basic sewing tools and supplies

Cutting

Step 1. Cut four 6½" x 44½" A strips gray print along length of fabric.

Step 2. Cut five 4½" x 44½" B strips black print along length of fabric.

Step 3. Cut five 2½" by fabric width strips burgundy mottled; join strips on short ends. Subcut strip into two 44½" C strips and two 48½" D strips.

Step 4. Cut the following 4½" x 4½" squares: 24 each dark green (E), cream (F) and black (G) prints and cream tonal (H) and eight each burgundy mottled (I) and red solid (J).

Step 5. Cut seven 3" by fabric width strips burgundy mottled for binding.

Appliquéd Strips

Step 1. Prepare templates for appliqué shapes using patterns given; cut as directed on each piece, adding a ⅛"–¼" seam allowance all around when cutting.

Step 2. Clip all curved seams on appliqué shapes.

Step 3. Cut one of each appliqué shape without seam allowance from heat-resistant template material.

Step 4. Spray edges of each fabric shape with spray sizing.

Step 5. Place a heat-resistant template in the center on the wrong side of a matching fabric shape. Iron the seam allowance to the wrong side of the fabric over the heat-resistant template edges; remove template and touch up fabric shape with the iron. Repeat for all fabric shapes.

Step 6. Prepare two 48½" lengths of ⅝"-wide bias from moss green mottled for vine.

Step 7. Prepare vine pieces for appliqué using heat-resistant template as in Step 5.

Step 8. Center and pin four pairs of holly leaves each with two burgundy mottled and two red solid holly berries across the width of an A strip referring to the Placement

DESIGN BY **JODI WARNER**

Holly Swirls

Holly-leaf shapes swirl on the blocks and borders of this hand-appliquéd wall quilt.

Project Specifications

Skill Level: Advanced

Quilt Size: 35" x 35"

Block Size: 6" x 6"

Number of Blocks: 8

Materials

- Scraps dark gold tonal and light gold solid
- Fat quarter red-and-cream print
- ½ yard red print
- ⅜ yard green tonal
- ⅜ yard green stripe
- ⅝ yard holiday print
- ⅝ yard red check
- Backing 41" x 41"
- Batting 41" x 41"
- All-purpose thread to match fabrics
- ⅜" circle punch (optional)
- Card stock
- Basic sewing tools and supplies and tweezers

Instructions

Step 1. Cut four 6½" x 6½" A squares red check. Fold each square in half diagonally and in half again; press to mark diagonal centers.

Step 2. Prepare templates for inner and outer holly leaf shapes using patterns given; cut as directed on each piece, adding a seam allowance when cutting for hand appliqué.

Figure 1
Transfer the holly-swirl design onto the right side of each A square.

Step 3. Using the holly-leaf templates, transfer the holly-swirl design onto the right side of each A square as shown in Figure 1.

Holly Swirl
6" x 6" Block

Holly Cluster
6" x 6" Block

Step 4. To prepare each leaf shape, fold the seam allowance under on the long curved edge of each inner-half leaf; baste to hold.

Step 5. Layer and pin the basted edge onto the corresponding outer-half leaf edge as shown in Figure 2. Hand-stitch pieces together along folded edge; remove basting.

Figure 2
Layer and pin the basted edge along the corresponding outer-half edge.

Figure 3
Position and pin 4 prepared leaves onto each A square.

Step 6. Fold seam allowance under and baste in place all around the stitched leaf shape, clipping into seam allowance at inner curves as necessary. Repeat to make 60 leaves.

Step 7. Position and pin four prepared leaves onto the transferred design on each A square as shown in Figure 3; appliqué edges in place. Remove basting; trim away excess A-square fabric from behind appliqués, leaving seam allowance.

Step 8. Punch 116 card-stock ⅜" circles (or photocopy multiple circle pattern onto card stock as directed and cut out). Prepare template for berry circle; cut as directed on pattern.

Step 9. With neutral color all-purpose thread in a hand-sewing needle, knot thread and baste from the right side around fabric circle within seam allowance as shown in Figure 4; leave needle and thread attached.

Figure 4
Baste from the right side
around fabric circle within
seam allowance.

Step 10. Place card-stock circle within basting against fabric circle wrong side as shown in Figure 5; pull threaded needle to gather fabric around card-stock circle, again referring to Figure 5. Backstitch to anchor; repeat to make 116 berries.

Figure 5
Place card-stock circle within basting against fabric
circle wrong side; pull threaded needle to gather fabric
around card-stock circle. Backstitch to anchor.

Step 11. Position a prepared berry on each A square referring to the block drawing for positioning; stitch in place with invisible stitches. Carefully cut an X through the back of the block behind the circle within stitching; remove card-stock form using tweezers as shown in Figure 6. Repeat to add four each light gold solid and dark gold tonal berries to each A square to complete the blocks.

Figure 6
Carefully cut an X through the
back of the block behind the circle
within stitching; remove card-stock
form using tweezers.

Step 12. Cut one 6½" x 6½" A, one 9¾" x 9¾" B and two 5⅛" x 5⅛" C squares from holiday print. Cut the B square on both diagonals to make four B triangles and the C squares on one diagonal to make four C triangles.

Step 13. Arrange the Holly Swirl blocks with the A, B and C pieces as shown in Figure 7. Join in diagonal rows and join rows to complete the quilt center.

Figure 7
Arrange the Holly Swirl
blocks with the A, B
and C pieces.

Step 14. Cut two 2" x 17½" D and two 2" x 20½" E strips red print. Sew D to opposite sides and E to the top and bottom of the quilt center; press seams toward D and E.

Step 15. Cut four 6½" x 20½" F rectangles red check. Fold each rectangle in half across width and in half again; press to mark four equal sections along length of F.

Step 16. Using the holly-leaf templates, transfer two holly-swag designs onto each F rectangle referring to Figure 8.

Step 17. Position, pin and appliqué prepared holly leaves on each F strip; hand-stitch in place. Remove basting;

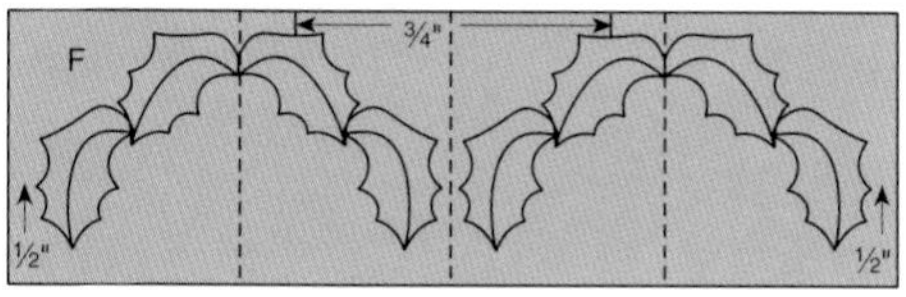

Figure 8
Transfer 2 holly-swag designs onto each F piece.

complete berry appliqué with 18 berries as in Step 11 and referring to the Placement Diagram for positioning.

Step 18. Cut four 6½" x 6½" G squares red-and-cream print; fold each on both diagonals; press to mark diagonal center. Using the holly-leaf templates, transfer holly-cluster design onto each square referring to Figure 9.

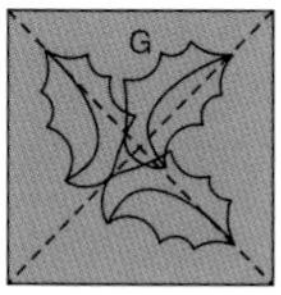

Figure 9
Transfer holly-cluster design onto each G square.

Step 19. Position, pin and appliqué prepared holly leaves on each G square. Remove basting; add three berries to complete the Holly Cluster blocks.

Step 20. Sew an F strip to opposite sides of the pieced center; press seams toward D. Sew a Holly Cluster block to each end of the remaining F strips; press seams toward blocks. Sew a strip to the top and bottom of the quilt center; press seams toward E.

Step 21. Cut two 2" x 32½" H and two 2" x 35½" I strips red print; sew H to opposite sides and I to the top and bottom of the quilt center; press seams toward H and I.

Step 22. Transfer crosshatch quilting design to the plain A square and B and C pieces as marked on pattern. Repeat with cable design on D, E, H and I strips and the ribbon designs on the F pieces and Holly Cluster blocks. Also mark 1" parallel lines behind the marked ribbon designs as shown in Figure 10.

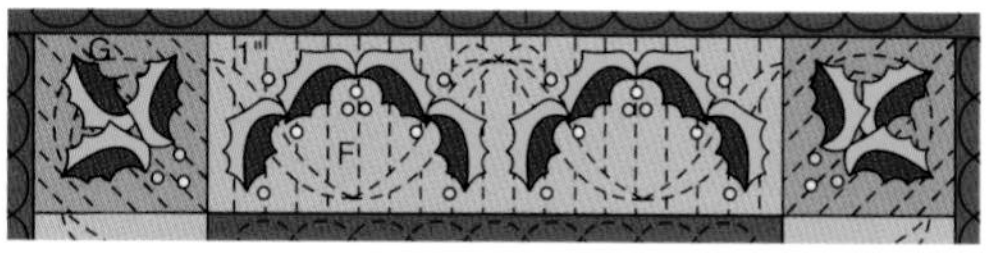

Figure 10
Mark 1" parallel lines on F and G.

Step 23. Sandwich the batting between the completed top and prepared backing; pin or baste layers together to hold.

Step 24. Hand-quilt on marked lines and around each appliqué shape. When quilting is complete, trim batting and backing even with top; remove pins or basting.

Step 25. Cut four 2¼" by fabric width strips holiday print for binding.

Step 26. Join the binding strips on short ends to make one long strip. Fold the strip in half along length with wrong sides together; press.

Step 27. Sew binding to quilt edges, mitering corners and overlapping ends. Fold binding to the back side and stitch in place. ❄

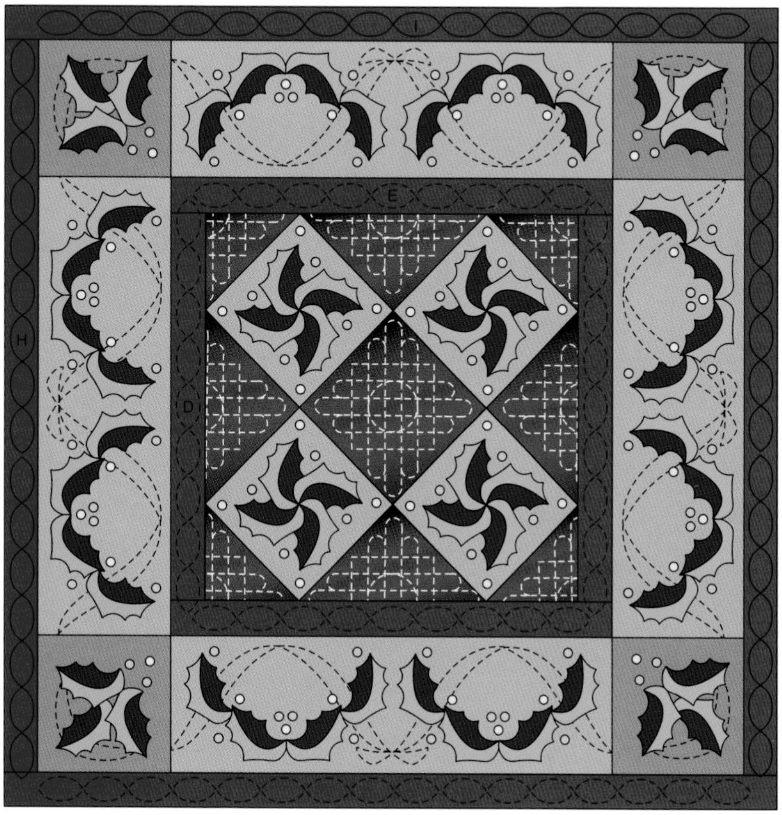

Holly Swirls
Placement Diagram
35" x 35"

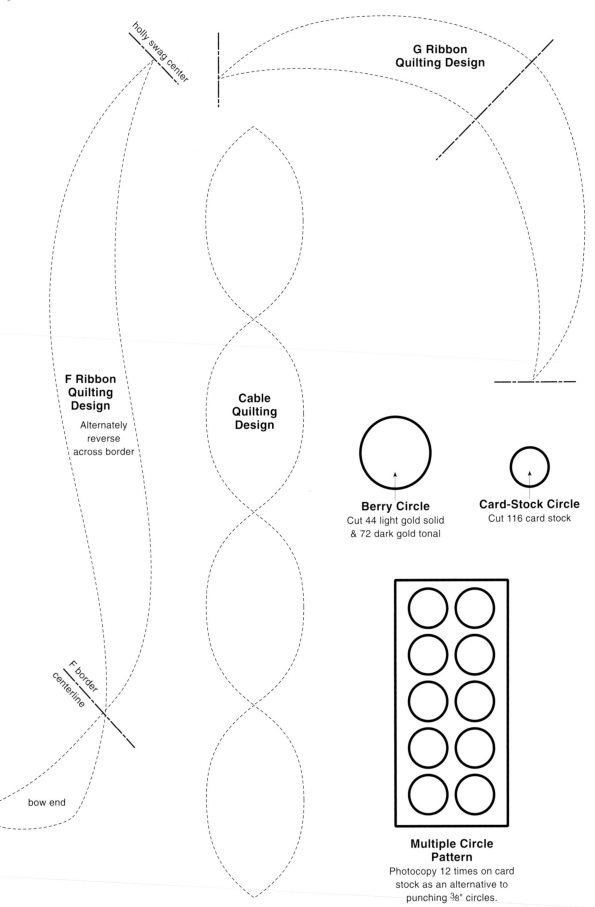

holly swag center

**G Ribbon
Quilting Design**

**F Ribbon
Quilting
Design**

Alternately
reverse
across border

**Cable
Quilting
Design**

Berry Circle
Cut 44 light gold solid
& 72 dark gold tonal

Card-Stock Circle
Cut 116 card stock

F border
centerline

bow end

**Multiple Circle
Pattern**
Photocopy 12 times on card
stock as an alternative to
punching ³⁄₈" circles.

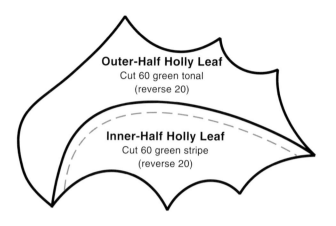

Outer-Half Holly Leaf
Cut 60 green tonal
(reverse 20)

Inner-Half Holly Leaf
Cut 60 green stripe
(reverse 20)

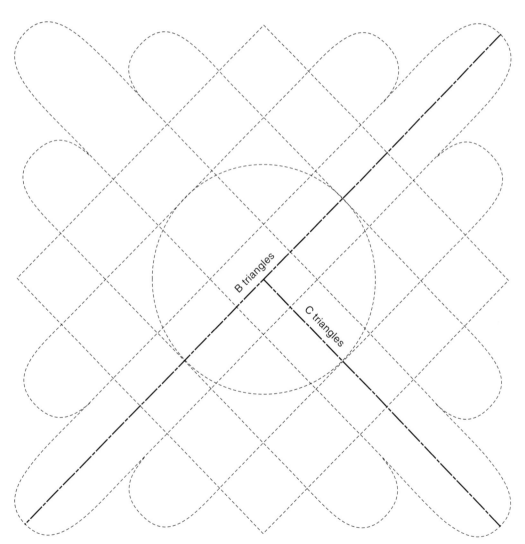

B triangles

C triangles

Crosshatch Quilting Design
Whole design for A, half design for B and
quarter design for C

Mother & Child

This small wall quilt tells the Christmas story in appliqué.

Project Specifications

Skill Level: Beginner
Quilt Size: 12¾" x 14"

Materials

- Scraps gold and light gold, light green, cream, peach and medium and dark purple mottleds for appliqué
- 6½" x 14" fabric strip for hanging sleeve
- 6¾" x 8" rectangle blue batik for A
- Fat quarter dark blue batik for B and C
- ¼ yard blue/purple batik for dress and binding
- Backing 19" x 20"
- Batting 19" x 20"
- Neutral color all-purpose thread
- Clear nylon monofilament
- Silver metallic thread
- ¼ yard fusible web
- Basic sewing tools and supplies

Instructions

Step 1. Trace each pattern shape onto the fusible web using pattern given. **Note:** *Pattern is given in reverse for fusible appliqué.*

Step 2. Cut out shapes leaving a margin around each one. Fuse shapes to the wrong side of fabrics as directed on patterns for color; cut out shapes on traced lines. Remove paper backing.

Step 3. Using the full-size pattern as a guide, arrange pieces (except star) on A in numerical order. When satisfied with placement, fuse shapes in place.

Step 4. Cut two 3¾" x 6¾" B strips and two 3¾" x 14½" C strips dark blue batik.

Step 5. Sew B to the top and bottom and C to opposite sides of the fused center; press seams toward B and C.

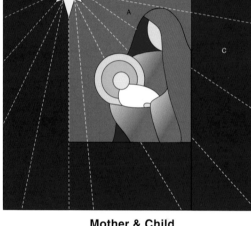

Mother & Child
Placement Diagram
12¾" x 14"

Step 6. Place the star in the upper left corner overlapping the B and C borders referring to the Placement Diagram for positioning; fuse in place.

Step 7. Sandwich the batting between the completed top and prepared backing; baste layers together.

Step 8. Using a small zigzag stitch and clear nylon monofilament, stitch around the mother/child motif pieces.

Step 9. Repeat Step 8 on star design using silver metallic thread.

Step 10. Machine-quilt radiating lines from the star using silver metallic thread and referring to the Placement Diagram for positioning.

Step 11. Cut two 2¼" by fabric width strips blue/purple batik; join strips on short ends to make one long binding strip. Fold the strip in half along length with wrong sides together; press.

Step 12. Sew binding to quilt edges, mitering corners and overlapping ends. Fold binding to the back side and stitch in place.

Step 13. Prepare hanging sleeve using the 6½" x 14" fabric strip and attach to the top back side of completed project being careful to keep stitching from showing on the right side. ❊

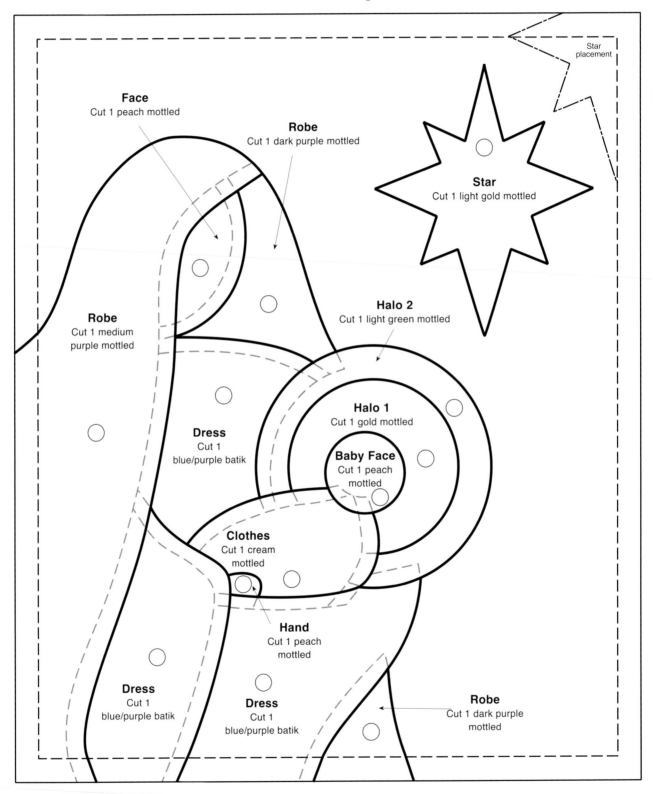

Face
Cut 1 peach mottled

Robe
Cut 1 dark purple mottled

Star
Cut 1 light gold mottled

Star placement

Robe
Cut 1 medium purple mottled

Halo 2
Cut 1 light green mottled

Halo 1
Cut 1 gold mottled

Dress
Cut 1 blue/purple batik

Baby Face
Cut 1 peach mottled

Clothes
Cut 1 cream mottled

Hand
Cut 1 peach mottled

Dress
Cut 1 blue/purple batik

Dress
Cut 1 blue/purple batik

Robe
Cut 1 dark purple mottled

Log Cabin Mantel Cover

The Log Cabin block design works perfectly to create this pretty mantel cover.

Project Specifications
Skill Level: Intermediate
Project Size: Approximately 45" x 14"
Block Size: 9" x 9"
Number of Blocks: 5

Materials
- 1 fat eighth each of 4 cream prints or tonals
- 1 fat eighth each of 2 green and 2 brown prints or tonals
- ⅜ yard burgundy tonal
- Backing 51" x 20"
- Batting 51" x 20"
- Neutral color all-purpose thread
- Quilting thread
- 5 (2½") burgundy tassels
- Basic sewing tools and supplies

Cutting
Step 1. Cut one 1½" x 22" strip burgundy tonal for piece 1.
Step 2. Cut five 1½" x 22" strips total from cream prints or tonals for light strips. Repeat with green and brown prints or tonals for dark strips.
Step 3. Cut four 2¼" by fabric width strips burgundy tonal for binding.

Piecing the Blocks
Step 1. Sew a light strip to the burgundy tonal strip with right sides together along length; press seams toward

Log Cabin
9" x 9" Block

burgundy tonal strip. Subcut strip set into eight 1½" units for piece 1-2 as shown in Figure 1.

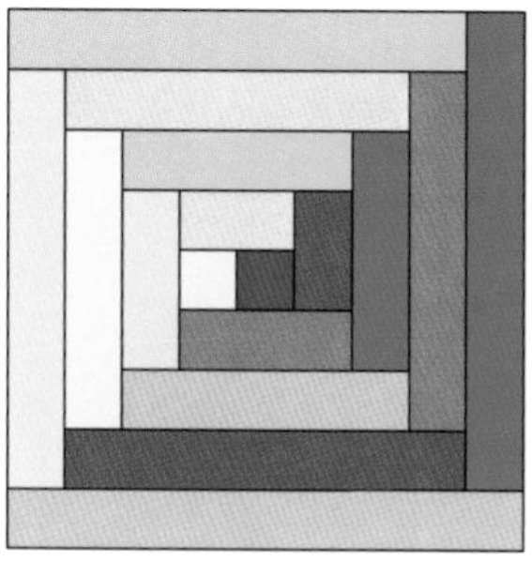

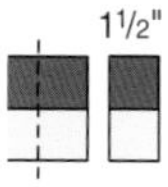

Figure 1
Subcut strip set into eight
1½" units for piece 1-2.

Figure 2
Sew the pieced units
to a light strip.

Step 2. Sew a 1-2 unit to a light strip as shown in Figure 2; press seams toward strip. Cut units apart as shown in Figure 3.

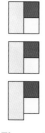

Figure 3
Cut units apart.

French Horn Place Mat

Hand appliqué using interfacing patterns creates perfect curved shapes.

Project Specifications
Skill Level: Intermediate
Quilt Size: 17" x 13"

Materials
- Scrap red solid
- Scraps gold mottled and yellow tonal
- ⅛ yard each red and light, medium and dark green tonals
- ½ yard dark green/black check
- Backing 23" x 19"
- Batting 23" x 19"
- All-purpose thread to match fabrics
- Yellow and dark green quilting thread
- ¼ yard interfacing
- Fabric glue stick
- Basic sewing tools and supplies

Cutting
Step 1. Cut an 11½" x 9½" A rectangle dark green/black check; fold and crease to mark the center.
Step 2. Cut two 2½" x 11½" B strips red tonal.
Step 3. Cut 24 dark green (C), 22 red (D), 14 medium green (E) and 12 light green (F) tonals and 6 dark green/black check (G) 1½" x 1½" squares.
Step 4. Cut two 2" x 17½" and two 2" x 14" binding strips dark green/black check.

Appliqué
Step 1. Trace each appliqué shape onto the interfacing using pattern given.

Step 2. Place the interfacing shapes traced side against the wrong side of fabrics as directed on each piece for color; use glue stick to secure pieces in place.
Step 3. Cut out shapes, adding ¼" around each shape beyond cut edge of interfacing. Mark detail lines on each piece referring to patterns.
Step 4. Clip fabric seam allowances every ¼" around all shapes. Apply glue to seam allowances and fold over the edges of the interfacing shapes, gluing fabric edges to the interfacing and being careful to preserve the design edge of each shape.
Step 5. Arrange the shapes on A in numerical order referring to the full-size pattern for placement, and matching center of design with center crease on A; hand-stitch each shape in place using matching all-purpose thread.

Completing the Top
Step 1. Sew a B strip to opposite long sides of the appliquéd center; press seams toward B.
Step 2. Join the C, D, E, F and G squares to make rows 1–3 as shown in Figure 1; repeat to make two rows each. Press seams in one direction, alternating the direction of row 2.

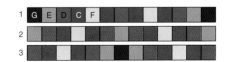

Figure 1
Join the C, D, E, F and G
squares to make rows 1–3.

DESIGN BY **JULIE WEAVER**

Blooming Christmas

A large floral print flannel adds richness to this warm bed-size quilt.

Project Specifications

Skill Level: Intermediate
Quilt Size: 68½" x 81"
Block Size: 10" x 10"
Number of Blocks: 20

Materials

Note: *All fabrics listed are flannel.*

- ⅓ yard 12 different prints
- ¾ yard cream floral
- 2 yards black large floral
- 2¾ yards black print
- Backing 75" x 87"
- Batting 75" x 87"
- Neutral color all-purpose thread
- Quilting thread
- Basic sewing tools and supplies

Project Note

Be very careful when joining sashing strips with D-E and D-E-F sashing units. It is important for the sashing units to be added in a specific way in order to create the woven look of the quilt.

Cutting

Step 1. Cut one 5½" by fabric width A strip from each of the 12 different prints; subcut strips into a total of (80) 5½" A squares.

Step 2. Cut one 3" by fabric width B strip from each of the 12 different prints; subcut strips into a total of (80) 3" B squares.

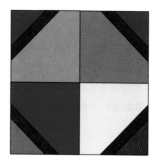

Divided Four-Patch
10" x 10" Block

Step 3. Cut eight 4" by fabric width C strips black print; subcut strips into (80) 4" C squares.

Step 4. Cut (15) 1½" by fabric width D strips cream floral.

Step 5. Cut (31) 1¼" by fabric width E strips black print.

Step 6. Cut two 8½" x 65½" G strips and two 8½" x 69" H strips along length of black large floral.

Step 7. Cut eight 2½" by fabric width strips black print for binding.

Making Blocks

Step 1. Draw a line from corner to corner on the wrong side of each B and C square.

Step 2. Place a C square right sides together on one corner of an A square as shown in Figure 1; stitch on the marked line, trim seam to ¼" and press C to the right side, again referring to Figure 1.

Figure 1
Place a C square right sides together on 1 corner of A; stitch on the marked line, trim seam to ¼" and press C to the right side.

DESIGN BY **CHRIS MALONE**

Denim Pals

Recycle those old jeans to make a warm holiday cover-up.

Project Specifications

Skill Level: Beginner
Quilt Size: 56" x 77"
Block Size: 7" x 7"
Number of Blocks: 88

Materials

- 12–14 pairs of recycled jeans or 4¼ yards new denim
- Scraps orange and brown flannel
- ¼ yard each cream, red, gold and green flannel
- 4¼ yards navy polka-dot flannel for backing
- 88 (6¾" x 6¾") squares batting
- All-purpose thread to match fabrics for appliqué
- Extra-strong denim-color and gold thread
- Fray preventative
- 12 (⅝") black buttons
- 12 (¼") black buttons
- 6 (⁹⁄₁₆") any color shank buttons
- 6 (⅝") red buttons
- 12 (⁹⁄₁₆") red buttons
- 3 (⅞") blue buttons
- Basic sewing tools and supplies

Instructions

Step 1. Prewash all flannel fabrics and denim or recycled jeans.

Step 2. Cut jeans apart along seams and cut as many 8" x 8" A blocks from each section as possible. **Note:** *A few blocks with pockets and other additions may be used as long as there is a margin of at least ¾" around pocket for seams.* Repeat for a total of 88 squares.

Step 3. Cut (88) 8" x 8" B squares from navy polka dot.

Step 4. Prepare templates for snowman, tree and star appliqué shapes and cut from fabrics as directed on each piece, adding a ⅛"–¼" seam allowance all around when cutting for hand appliqué.

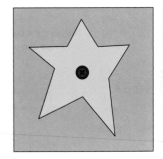

Snowman
7" x 7" Block

Star
7" x 7" Block

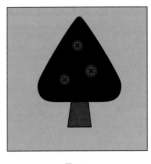

Tree
7" x 7" Block

Step 5. Center a star shape on one A block; turn under seam allowance and hand-stitch in place. Repeat for three Star blocks.

Step 6. Center a snowman shape with scarf and nose pieces on one A block; turn under seam allowances and hand-stitch pieces in place. Repeat for six Snowman blocks. **Note:** *Switch the positioning of the nose to make three right- and three left-facing snowmen.*

Step 7. Arrange a tree with trunk on one A block; appliqué trunk first and then tree as for other blocks. Repeat for six tree blocks.

Step 8. Mark a star design on each plain A square for quilting later.

Step 9. Place a B square wrong side up on a flat surface; center a batting square on top. Place an appliqué block

DESIGN BY **CONNIE RAND**

Christmas Flowers

Strategic placement of blocks creates a subtle design in this bed-size holiday quilt.

Project Specifications
Skill Level: Intermediate
Quilt Size: 83" x 97½"
Block Size: 12" x 12"
Number of Blocks: 30

Materials
- 1¼ yards green holly print
- 2⅛ yards gold print
- 2⅞ yards black holly print
- 2⅞ yards green tonal
- 2⅞ yards red solid
- Backing 89" x 104"
- Batting 89" x 104"
- All-purpose thread to match fabrics
- Quilting thread
- Basic sewing tools and supplies

Cutting
Step 1. Prepare templates using pattern pieces given: cut as directed on each piece.
Step 2. Cut nine 3" by fabric width strips gold print; subcut strips into (120) 3" E squares.
Step 3. Cut three 3" by fabric width strips red solid; subcut strips into (42) 3" F squares.
Step 4. Cut six 12½" by fabric width strips green tonal; subcut strips into (71) 3" G segments for sashing strips.
Step 5. Cut nine 4½" by fabric width strips gold print. Join strips on short ends to make one long strip; subcut strip into two 4½" x 90" H strips and two 4½" x 83½" I strips.

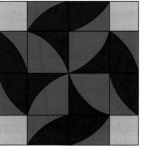

Christmas Flowers 1
12" x 12" Block

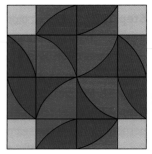

Christmas Flowers 2
12" x 12" Block

Step 6. Cut nine 2¼" by fabric width strips green tonal for binding.

Completing the Blocks
Step 1. To piece one Christmas Flowers 1 block, sew A to a black holly print B, matching notches; press seams toward A. Repeat for four A-B units. Join units as shown in Figure 1; press seams toward A.

Figure 1
Sew A to B; join 4
units as shown.

Figure 2
Sew C to D; join
2 units as shown.

Step 2. Sew a black holly print C to D, matching notches; press seam toward C. Repeat for eight C-D units.
Step 3. Join two C-D units as shown in Figure 2; press seam in one direction. Repeat for four units.

Step 4. Sew a C-D unit to each side of an A-B unit as shown in Figure 3; press seams toward the A-B unit.

Figure 3
Sew a C-D unit to each
side of an A-B unit.

Step 5. Sew E to each end of the remaining C-D units referring to Figure 4; press seams toward E.

Figure 4
Sew E to each end of
a C-D unit as shown.

Step 6. Join the C-D-E units with the previously pieced unit to complete one Christmas Flowers 1 block as shown in Figure 5; press seams toward C-D-E. Repeat for 22 Christmas Flowers 1 blocks. Repeat to make eight Christmas Flowers 2 blocks using green holly print for B and C pieces, again referring to Figure 5.

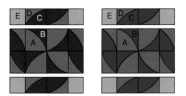

Figure 5
Join units to complete Christmas
Flowers 1 and 2 blocks.

Completing the Top

Step 1. Join six F squares with five G strips to make a sashing row as shown in Figure 6. Repeat for seven sashing rows; press seams toward G.

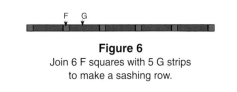

Figure 6
Join 6 F squares with 5 G strips
to make a sashing row.

Step 2. Join five blocks with six G strips to make a block row as shown in Figure 7; repeat for six block rows. Press seams toward F.

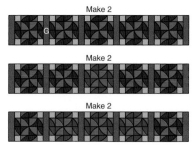

Figure 7
Join 5 blocks with 6 G strips to
make a block row.

Step 3. Join the block rows with the sashing rows to complete the pieced center referring to the Placement Diagram for positioning of rows; press seams in one direction.

Step 4. Sew H strips to opposite sides and I strips to the top and bottom of the pieced center; press seams toward H and I to complete the top.

Finishing the Quilt

Step 1. Sandwich the batting between the completed top

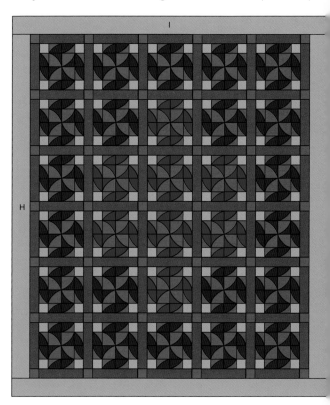

Christmas Flowers
Placement Diagram
83" x 97½"

and prepared backing; pin or baste layers together to hold.
Step 2. Quilt as desired by hand or machine. When quilting is complete, trim batting and backing even with top; remove pins or basting.
Step 3. Join binding strips on short ends to make one long strip. Fold the strip in half along length with wrong sides together; press.
Step 4. Sew binding to quilt edges, mitering corners and overlapping ends. Fold binding to the back side and stitch in place. ❊

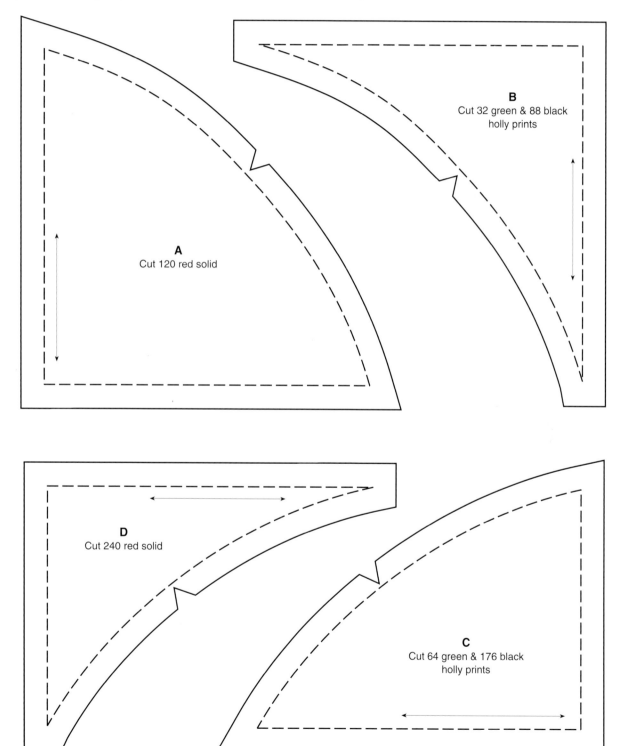

A
Cut 120 red solid

B
Cut 32 green & 88 black holly prints

D
Cut 240 red solid

C
Cut 64 green & 176 black holly prints

Sampler Christmas Stocking

Embroidered snowflakes, tiny Star blocks and appliquéd hearts send a holiday message on this pretty stocking.

Project Specifications
Skill Level: Intermediate
Stocking Size: 16½" long
Block Size: 2" x 2"
Number of Blocks: 3

Materials
- I fat quarter muslin
- ¼ yard total red scraps
- I yard red print
- Batting 18" x 40"
- Neutral color all-purpose thread
- Red 6-strand embroidery floss
- Freezer paper
- Washable marking pen or fine-point permanent red fabric marker
- Basic sewing tools and supplies and press cloth

Making Star Strip
Step 1. Cut one each 2½" x 8½" and 3" x 8½" strips muslin; set aside for snowflake and heart rows. Cut (12) 1" x 1" B squares, two 1¼" x 2½" D strips and two ¾" x 2½" E strips muslin.

Step 2. Cut four 1½" x 10" bias strips each of red scraps and muslin.

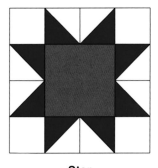

Star
2" x 2" Block

Step 3. Join one each muslin and red scrap bias strips using a ⅛" seam allowance with right sides together along length as shown in Figure 1; press seams toward red strip. Angle ends, again referring to Figure 1. Repeat for four strip sets.

Figure 1
Join muslin and bias strips; angle ends.

Figure 2
Align the 45-degree-angle line on the ruler with the seam in the strip set and rough-cut a 1" square.

Step 4. Using a square rotary-cutting ruler, align the 45-degree-angle line on the ruler with the seam in a strip set and rough-cut a 1" square as shown in Figure 2. Turn square 180 degrees and trim the square so it measures exactly 1" x 1"; repeat for 24 A squares.

Step 5. Cut three different 1½" × 1½" C squares from red scraps.

Step 6. Using a ¼" seam allowance throughout block piecing, join two A squares with two B squares to make a row as shown in Figure 3; repeat for two rows. Press A seams open and remaining seams toward B.

Figure 3
Join 2 A squares with 2 B squares to make a row.

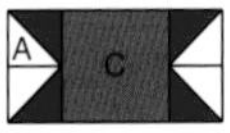

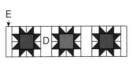

Figure 4
Sew an A unit to opposite sides of C.

Step 7. Join two A squares; press seam open. Repeat for two units. Sew an A unit to opposite sides of C as shown in Figure 4; press seams toward C.

Step 8. Join the pieced units to complete a Star block as shown in Figure 5; repeat for three Star blocks.

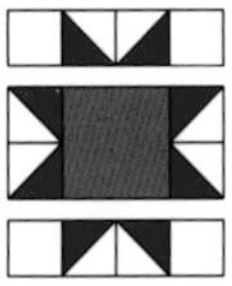

Figure 5
Join the pieced units to complete a Star block.

Figure 6
Join the 3 blocks with the D and E strips to complete the star strip.

Step 9. Join the three blocks with the D and E strips to complete the star strip as shown in Figure 6; press seams toward D and E.

Making Snowflake Strip

Step 1. Fold the 2½" × 8½" muslin strip to find the center and crease. Using a washable marking pen or fine-point permanent red fabric marker, center and transfer one snowflake design given onto the muslin strip. Repeat on each side of the marked motif, leaving ½" between motifs.

Step 2. Using 1 strand red embroidery floss and referring to snowflake pattern for stitching suggestions, complete embroidery.

Step 3. Press embroidered strip on the wrong side using a press cloth.

Making Heart Strip

Step 1. Using heart pattern provided, trace three hearts on the dull side of freezer paper.

Step 2. Cut out hearts on drawn line. Iron freezer-paper

hearts, shiny side down, to the wrong side of three red scraps. Cut out hearts, leaving ³⁄₁₆" turn-under seam allowance.

Step 3. Fold the 3" × 8½" muslin strip to find the center and crease. Center hearts on the muslin strip no more than ⅜" apart; hand-appliqué in place.

Step 4. Cut a hole behind each heart shape on the wrong side of the strip; remove freezer paper. Press completed strip.

Stocking Assembly

Step 1. Cut two 1" × 8½" F strips red print. Join the completed strips with F as shown in Figure 7; press seams toward F.

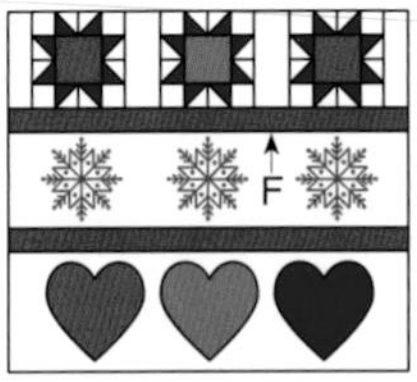

Figure 7
Join the completed strips with F.

Figure 8
Complete the stocking front as shown.

Step 2. Using the pattern provided, cut stocking lower front from red print.

Step 3. Sew the pieced strip section to the top edge of the stocking lower front to complete the stocking front as shown in Figure 8; press seam toward stocking lower front.

Step 4. Cut backing, lining and batting pieces as directed on pattern.

Step 5. Layer stocking front and back pieces separately with batting and quilt as desired. **Note:** *The sample was hand-quilted in the ditch of strip seams, around appliquéd hearts and in a marked design as shown on the stocking pattern.*

Step 6. Lay back lining piece and quilted stocking back right sides together, aligning at top edge. Stitch across top edge with a ¼" seam allowance. Press seam open, turn lining to back and press along seam at top edge.

Step 7. For stocking front lining, trim batting at top edge of stocking front ¼" above raw edge of star strip; lay the front lining piece right sides together with quilted stocking front so top raw edge is aligned with raw edge of star strip. Sew a ¼" seam along top edge as shown in Figure 9.

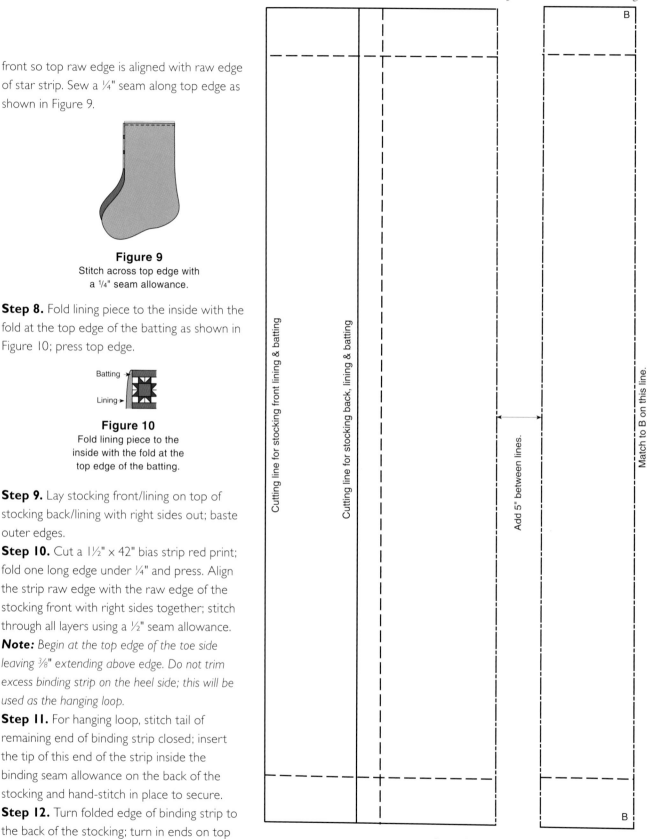

Figure 9
Stitch across top edge with
a ¼" seam allowance.

Step 8. Fold lining piece to the inside with the fold at the top edge of the batting as shown in Figure 10; press top edge.

Figure 10
Fold lining piece to the
inside with the fold at the
top edge of the batting.

Step 9. Lay stocking front/lining on top of stocking back/lining with right sides out; baste outer edges.

Step 10. Cut a 1½" x 42" bias strip red print; fold one long edge under ¼" and press. Align the strip raw edge with the raw edge of the stocking front with right sides together; stitch through all layers using a ½" seam allowance. **Note:** *Begin at the top edge of the toe side leaving ⅜" extending above edge. Do not trim excess binding strip on the heel side; this will be used as the hanging loop.*

Step 11. For hanging loop, stitch tail of remaining end of binding strip closed; insert the tip of this end of the strip inside the binding seam allowance on the back of the stocking and hand-stitch in place to secure.

Step 12. Turn folded edge of binding strip to the back of the stocking; turn in ends on top toe side, hand-stitch in place on top edge and back of stocking to finish. ❈

Cutting line for stocking front lining & batting

Cutting line for stocking back, lining & batting

Add 5" between lines.

Match to B on this line.

B

B

Stocking
Cut 1 stocking lower front red print
Cut 1 stocking back lining red print & batting;
reverse & cut 1 stocking back red print
Reverse & cut 1 stocking lining red print & batting

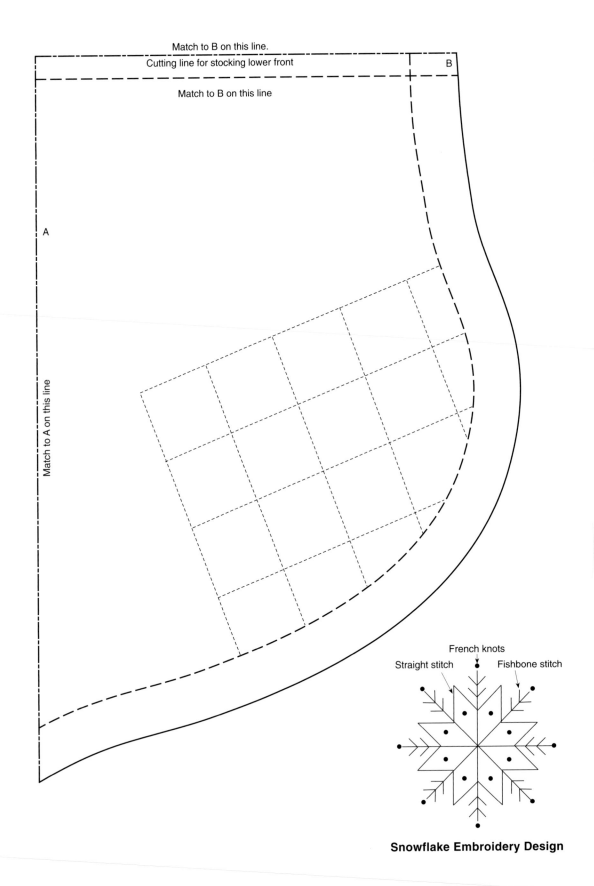

Match to B on this line.

Cutting line for stocking lower front

Match to B on this line

A

Match to A on this line

B

French knots

Straight stitch   Fishbone stitch

Snowflake Embroidery Design

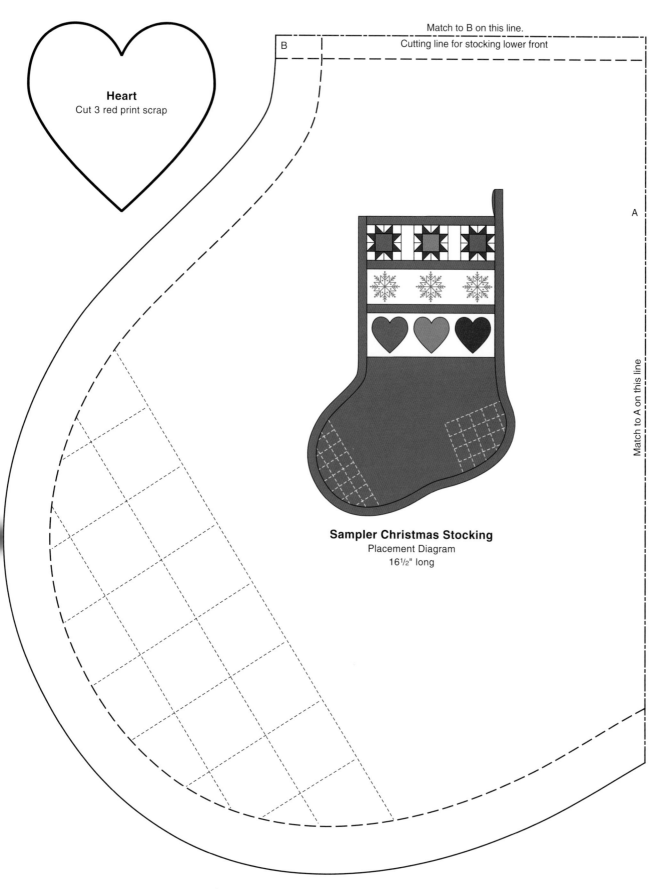

Match to B on this line.

B

Cutting line for stocking lower front

A

Match to A on this line

Heart
Cut 3 red print scrap

Sampler Christmas Stocking
Placement Diagram
16½" long

Light of the World

A simple pieced eight-pointed star is vibrant in red and white fabrics.

Project Specifications
Skill Level: Intermediate
Quilt Size: 30¾" x 30¾"

Materials
- 6⅞" x 6⅞" square thin white solid
- ⅛ yard red/black print
- ¼ yard red/white print
- ¼ yard red paisley tonal
- ½ yard cream mottled
- 1 yard red print
- Backing 37" x 37"
- Batting 37" x 37"
- All-purpose thread to match fabrics
- Red quilting thread
- Red 6-strand embroidery floss
- Heat-proof template plastic
- Basic sewing tools and supplies

Cutting
Step 1. Cut the following 2" by fabric width strips: one cream mottled (A); two red/white print (B); three red paisley tonal (C); two red print (D); and one red/black print (E).
Step 2. Cut nine 6⅞" x 6⅞" F squares cream mottled.
Step 3. Prepare template for G using pattern given; cut as directed on the piece.
Step 4. Cut four 2¼" by fabric width strips red print for binding.

Completing the Top
Step 1. Join strips with right sides together along length in the following combinations and referring to Figure 1: A, B and C; B, C and D; and C, D and E. Press seams in one direction.

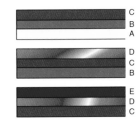

Figure 1
Join strips in
combinations shown.

Step 2. Cut eight 2" segments from each strip set at a 45-degree angle as shown in Figure 2.

Figure 2
Cut 2" segments at a
45-degree angle.

Figure 3
Join 1 segment of
each combination to
make a star point.

Step 3. Join one segment of each combination to make a star point as shown in Figure 3; repeat for eight star points. Press seams in one direction.
Step 4. Join star points in pairs, stopping stitching at the

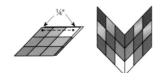

Figure 4
Join star points in pairs,
stopping stitching at the
seam end, not at the
end of the piece.

seam end, not at the end of the piece, as shown in Figure 4. Repeat to join pairs to make half of the star motif; repeat for two halves. Join the halves to complete the star shape; press seams in one direction and the center points open as shown in Figure 5.

Figure 5
Press the center
point seams open.

Figure 6
Set an F square into opening
between star points.

Step 5. Set an F square into opening between star points as shown in Figure 6; press seams toward F.

Step 6. Make a cardboard or heat-proof plastic circle template 4¼" in diameter. Layer the thin white solid square with the remaining F square; cut a 4½" circle. **Note:** *You may use the template circle, but add ⅛" all around.*

Step 7. Center and transfer the embroidery design given onto the F circle.

Step 8. Using 3 strands red embroidery floss and a stem stitch, stitch on the marked lines through both layers. Press stitched design from the wrong side.

Step 9. Baste around the edge of the embroidered circle 1/8" from edge, knotting the end. Lay the circle template on the wrong side of the embroidered fabric circle and pull the basting thread to cinch fabric around template as shown in Figure 7; press from the wrong side.

Figure 7
Pull the basting
thread to cinch fabric
around template.

Step 10. Remove the template. Center and hand-stitch the circle over the center of the pieced star.

Step 11. Trim away the pieced star from behind the appliquéd circle to reduce bulk.

Step 12. Set G pieces between F squares as shown in Figure 8 to complete the pieced top; press seams toward G.

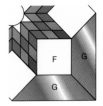

Figure 8
Set G pieces
between F squares.

Finishing the Quilt

Step 1. Mark the quilting design given onto the F squares.

Step 2. Sandwich batting between the completed top and prepared backing; pin or baste to hold layers together.

Step 3. Quilt in the ditch of star design using white quilting thread and on the marked quilting design using red quilting thread.

Step 4. When quilting is complete, trim batting and backing even with quilt top.

Step 5. Join the binding strips on short ends to make one long strip. Fold the strip in half along length with wrong sides together; press.

Step 6. Sew binding to quilt edges, mitering corners and overlapping ends. Fold binding to the back side and stitch in place. ❄

Quilting Design

Light of the World
Placement Diagram
30¾" x 30¾"

Place line on fold

G
Cut 8 red print

Embroidery Design

Christmas Puzzle

Color placement creates the look of an interlocking design in this pretty holiday quilt.

Project Specifications

Skill Level: Beginner
Quilt Size: 78" x 98"
Block Size: 12" x 8"
Number of Blocks: 50

Materials

- 1⅝ yards dark red tonal
- 2⅛ yards dark green tonal
- 2½ yards cream tonal
- 4¼ yards holiday check
- Backing 84" x 104"
- Batting 84" x 104"
- All-purpose thread to match fabrics
- Quilting thread
- Basic sewing tools and supplies

Cutting

Step 1. Cut seven 4½" by fabric width strips each holiday check (A), dark red tonal (B) cream tonal (C) and dark green tonal (D); subcut strips into (100) 2½" rectangles each A, B, C and D.

Step 2. Cut seven 2½" by fabric width strips each holiday check (E), dark red tonal (F), cream tonal (G) and dark green tonal (H).

Step 3. Cut eight 3½" by fabric width strips cream tonal; join strips on short ends to make one long strip. Subcut strip into two 60½" I strips and two 86½" J strips.

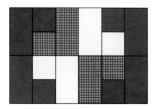

Christmas Puzzle
12" x 8" Block

Step 4. Cut two 6½" x 66½" K strips and two 6½" x 98½" L strips along the length of the holiday check.

Step 5. Cut nine 2¼" by fabric width strips dark green tonal for binding.

Completing the Blocks

Step 1. Sew an H strip to an E strip with right sides together along length; press seams toward H. Repeat for seven strip sets. Subcut strip sets into (100) 2½" E-H units as shown in Figure 1. Repeat with F and G strips to make 100 F-G units, again referring to Figure 1.

Figure 1
Subcut strip sets
into 2½" units to
make E-H and
F-G units.

Step 2. Sew A to one side and D to the opposite side of an E-H unit as shown in Figure 2; repeat for 100 units. Press seams toward E-H.

Figure 2
Sew A and D
to an E-H unit.

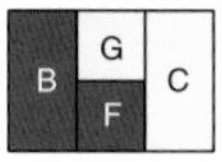

Figure 3
Sew B and C to
an F-G unit.

Step 3. Sew B to one side and C to the opposite side of an F-G unit as shown in Figure 3; repeat for 100 units. Press seams toward B and C.

Step 4. Join one B-F-G-C unit with one D-E-H-A unit as shown in Figure 4; press seams toward A. Repeat for 100 units.

Figure 4
Join 2 units
as shown.

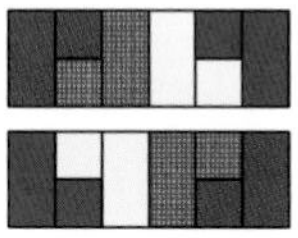

Figure 5
Join units to
complete 1 block.

Step 5. Join two pieced units to complete one block as shown in Figure 5; repeat for 50 blocks. Press seams in one direction.

Completing the Top
Step 1. Join five blocks on the short ends to make a row as shown in Figure 6; repeat for 10 rows. Press seams in one direction.

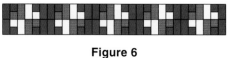

Figure 6
Join 5 blocks to make a row.

Step 2. Join rows with seams of adjacent rows pressed in opposite directions; press seams in one direction.
Step 3. Sew an I strip to the top and bottom and J strips to opposite sides of the pieced center; press seams toward I and J.

Step 4. Sew a K strip to the top and bottom and L strips to opposite sides of the pieced center; press seams toward K and L.

Finishing the Quilt
Step 1. Sandwich batting between the completed top and prepared backing; pin or baste to hold layers together.
Step 2. Quilt as desired by hand or machine; remove pins or basting.
Step 3. When quilting is complete, trim batting and backing even with quilt top.
Step 4. Join the binding strips on short ends to make one long strip. Fold the strip in half along length with wrong sides together; press.
Step 5. Sew binding to quilt edges, mitering corners and overlapping ends. Fold binding to the back side and stitch in place. ✲

Christmas Puzzle
Placement Diagram
78" x 98"

Holly Jolly Basket

This basket is full of holly leaves to add to your holly jolly Christmas.

Project Specifications
Skill Level: Intermediate
Quilt Size: 26½" x 26½"
Block Size: 12" x 12"
Number of Blocks: 1

Materials
- Scraps red and green prints for basket
- 8" x 8" square red print for bow
- ⅛ yard dark green print for holly leaves
- ⅛ yard gold lamé for borders
- ¼ yard red print for borders
- ¼ yard red mottled for binding
- ⅜ yard green print for borders
- ½ yard white-with-gold print for background
- Backing 32" x 32"
- Batting 32" x 32"
- All-purpose thread to match fabrics
- Quilting thread
- 1 package ½"-wide gold lamé bias tape
- 1 yard fusible web
- Fabric glue
- 22 small red pompoms
- Basic sewing tools and supplies

Cutting
Step 1. Cut one 12⅞" x 12⅞" square white-with-gold print; cut the square on one diagonal to make the A triangle. Use remaining triangle for block I and K pieces.

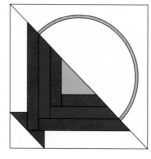

Holly Jolly Basket
12" x 12" Block

Step 2. Prepare templates for basket pieces using patterns given; cut as directed on each piece.
Step 3. Prepare templates for holly leaf and bow using patterns given; trace 20 holly leaves and one bow shape onto the paper side of the fusible web.
Step 4. Cut out shapes, leaving a margin around each one; fuse holly leaf shapes to the wrong side of the dark green print and bow shape to the wrong side of the 8" x 8" square red print. Cut out shapes on traced lines; remove paper backing.
Step 5. Cut four 1¾" x 17" L strips gold lamé.
Step 6. Cut two 11⅜" x 11⅜" squares white-with-gold print; cut each square in half on one diagonal to make M triangles.
Step 7. Cut two 1¼" x 21½" N strips and two 1¼" x 23" O strips red print.
Step 8. Cut four 2½" x 29" P strips green print.
Step 9. Cut three 2¼" by fabric width strips red mottled for binding.

Piecing the Basket Block

Step 1. Sew C to B and add D as shown in Figure 1; press seams toward C and D. Continue adding strips E–H in alphabetical order, referring to Figure 2; press seam toward each newly added strip after stitching.

Figure 1
Sew C to B
and add D.

Figure 2
Add pieces in
alphabetical order.

Step 2. Sew J to I as shown in Figure 3; repeat for a reversed I-J unit, again referring to Figure 3. Press seams toward J.

Figure 3
Sew J to I; repeat for
a reversed I-J unit.

Step 3. Sew the I-J units to the previously pieced unit as shown in Figure 4; press seam toward I-J.

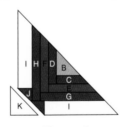

Figure 4
Sew the I-J units to the
previously pieced unit. Add K
to the corner to complete the
pieced half of the block.

Step 4. Add K to the corner to complete the pieced half of the block, again referring to Figure 4; press seam toward K.

Step 5. Fold A to find the center of the diagonal edge. Cut an 18" length of ½"-wide gold lamé bias tape. Measure in 3½" from each diagonal edge and mark with a pin. Align the edge of each end of the bias tape with the pin and pin in place. Arrange the bias tape in a pleasing curve, making the highest point of the curve match the center crease of A as shown in Figure 5.

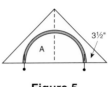

Figure 5
Center handle on
A with ends 3½"
from each side.

Step 6. When satisfied with placement of bias tape handle, hand-stitch in place with matching all-purpose thread.
Step 7. Stitch the A handle piece to the pieced bottom section to complete the basket block as shown in Figure 6; press seam away from A.

Figure 6
Join the units to
complete the block.

Holly Jolly Basket
Placement Diagram
26½" x 26½"

Completing the Top

Step 1. Center and sew an L strip to each side of the pieced block, mitering corners. Trim corner seams to ¼" and press open. Press seams toward L.

Step 2. Sew an M triangle to two opposite sides of the pieced center; press seams toward M.

Step 3. Sew the remaining M triangles to the remaining sides of the pieced center; press seams toward M. **Note:** *The M triangles will overlap at the edges as shown in Figure 7.*

Figure 7
M triangles overlap
at edges.

Step 4. Sew an N strip to the top and bottom and an O strip to opposite sides of the pieced center; press seams toward N and O.

Step 5. Center and sew a P strip to each side of the pieced center, mitering corners. Trim corner seams to ¼" and press open. Press seams toward P.

Step 6. Center and fuse a cluster of three holly leaves in each M triangle referring to Figure 8 for overlapping of leaves.

Figure 8
Center and fuse a cluster of 3
holly leaves in each M triangle.

Step 7. Arrange the remaining holly leaves on the pieced basket block referring to the Placement Diagram for positioning. When satisfied with arrangement, fuse in place.

Step 8. Fuse the bow shape onto the handle area of the pieced basket block referring to the Placement Diagram for positioning.

Step 9. Machine-appliqué leaves and bow in place using matching all-purpose thread and a medium-width zigzag stitch.

Finishing the Quilt

Step 1. Sandwich batting between the completed top and prepared backing; pin or baste to hold layers together.

Step 2. Quilt as desired by hand or machine.

Step 3. When quilting is complete, trim batting and backing even with quilt top.

Step 4. Join the binding strips on short ends to make one long strip. Fold the strip in half along length with wrong sides together; press.

Step 5. Sew binding to quilt edges, mitering corners and overlapping ends. Fold binding to the back side and stitch in place. **Note:** *A hanging sleeve may be added to the top back side of the quilt, if desired.*

Step 6. Arrange a cluster of three red pompoms at the base of each leaf cluster and one on the single leaf; glue in place with fabric glue to finish. ❈

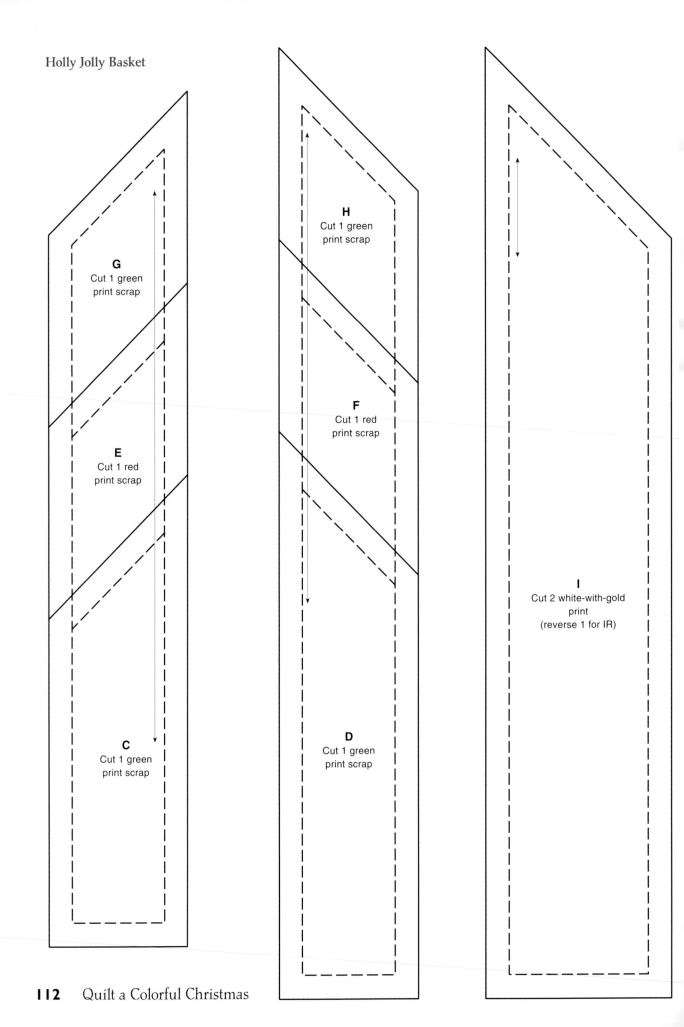

G
Cut 1 green
print scrap

E
Cut 1 red
print scrap

C
Cut 1 green
print scrap

H
Cut 1 green
print scrap

F
Cut 1 red
print scrap

D
Cut 1 green
print scrap

I
Cut 2 white-with-gold
print
(reverse 1 for IR)

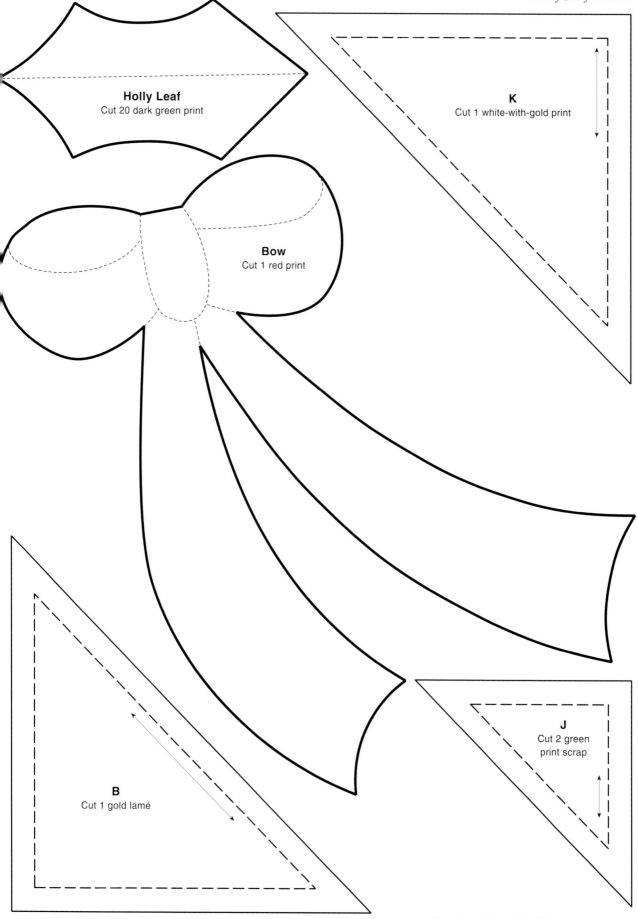

Holly Leaf
Cut 20 dark green print

K
Cut 1 white-with-gold print

Bow
Cut 1 red print

B
Cut 1 gold lamé

J
Cut 2 green print scrap

Wreath of Plenty

Decorate your door with a fabric wreath during the holiday season.

Project Specifications

Skill Level: Intermediate
Quilt Size: 24" x 24"

Materials

- Scraps maroon, scarlet, gold and purple mottleds
- Fat quarter dark green mottled
- ⅜ yard medium green mottled
- 26" x 26" square white solid for background
- ½ yard burgundy metallic for binding
- Backing 30" x 30"
- Batting 30" x 30"
- All-purpose thread to match fabrics
- Red and white quilting thread
- Brown 6-strand embroidery floss
- 1 sheet heat-resistant template material
- Spray sizing
- Basic sewing tools and supplies

Instructions

Step 1. Cut a 13" x 13" square medium green mottled; fold in quarters and press.

Step 2. Trace the ¼ under wreath pattern onto the fabric as shown in Figure 1; mark and cut. Open wreath circle and press flat.

Step 3. Fold the 26" x 26" background square in quarters and crease to mark the center; open and place on a flat surface.

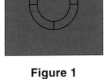

Figure 1
Trace the ¼ under wreath pattern onto the fabric.

Step 4. Center the wreath circle on the background square, matching the pressed fold lines; pin or baste to hold. Turn under raw edges of wreath circle ¼" while appliquéing in place using all-purpose thread to match fabric.

Step 5. Prepare templates for leaves and fruits; trace patterns onto heat-resistant template material without seams.

Step 6. Trace shapes onto fabrics referring to patterns for color and number to cut and adding a ⅛"–¼" seam allowance all around for hand appliqué.

Step 7. Apply light coating of sizing spray to the outside edges of all pieces except berries. Place each piece right side down on a towel or other work surface. Center the corresponding template on one piece and turn the appliqué seam over the template; press firmly with an iron. Gently remove the template and repeat process with each piece.

Step 8. Baste around each berry circle on the marked seam allowance with a knotted thread. Pull the thread to cinch the berry into a circle as shown in Figure 2; knot thread and iron. Repeat for all berries.

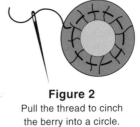

Figure 2
Pull the thread to cinch the berry into a circle.

Step 9. Arrange and hand-stitch the prepared appliqué shapes on the wreath circle with matching all-purpose thread, working from the outside in and referring to the

Placement Diagram and project photo for positioning suggestions. **Note:** *The fabric wreath should be covered as much as possible by appliqué shapes.* Add berries last.

Step 10. Stem-stitch a freehand stem on each pear and apple using 3 strands brown embroidery floss.

Step 11. Trim appliquéd square to 24½" × 24½". Sandwich batting between the completed top and prepared backing; pin or baste to hold layers together.

Step 12. Transfer the heart quilting design to the center of the wreath and a single heart in each corner. Quilt on traced lines and echo-quilt around outer edges of the wreath in lines ½" apart using white quilting thread and on the marked quilting design using red quilting thread.

Step 13. When quilting is complete, trim batting and backing even with quilt top.

Step 14. Cut three 4½" by fabric width strips burgundy metallic for binding. Join the binding strips on short ends to make one long strip. Press in half along length with wrong sides together.

Step 15. Pin binding with raw edges even with quilt edges; stitch all around, mitering corners and overlapping ends. Fold binding to the back side and stitch in place.

Note: *A hanging sleeve may be added to the top back side of the quilt, if desired.* ❄

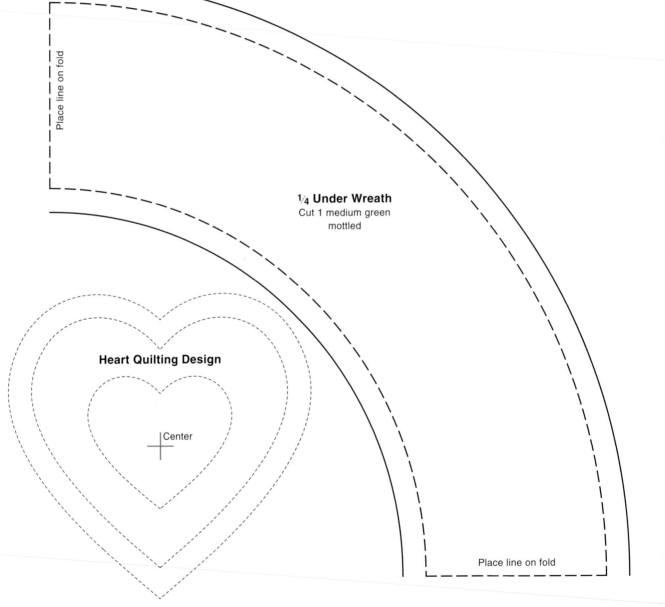

Place line on fold

¼ **Under Wreath**
Cut 1 medium green
mottled

Heart Quilting Design

Center

Place line on fold

Plum
Cut 2 purple scrap

Holly Leaf
Cut 9 dark green
mottled

Add ¼" seam allowance
all around when cutting
for hand appliqué.

Large Leaf
Cut 24 medium
green mottled

Apple
Cut 2 maroon scrap

Berry
← Cut 10
scarlet scrap

Small Leaf
Cut 15 medium
green mottled

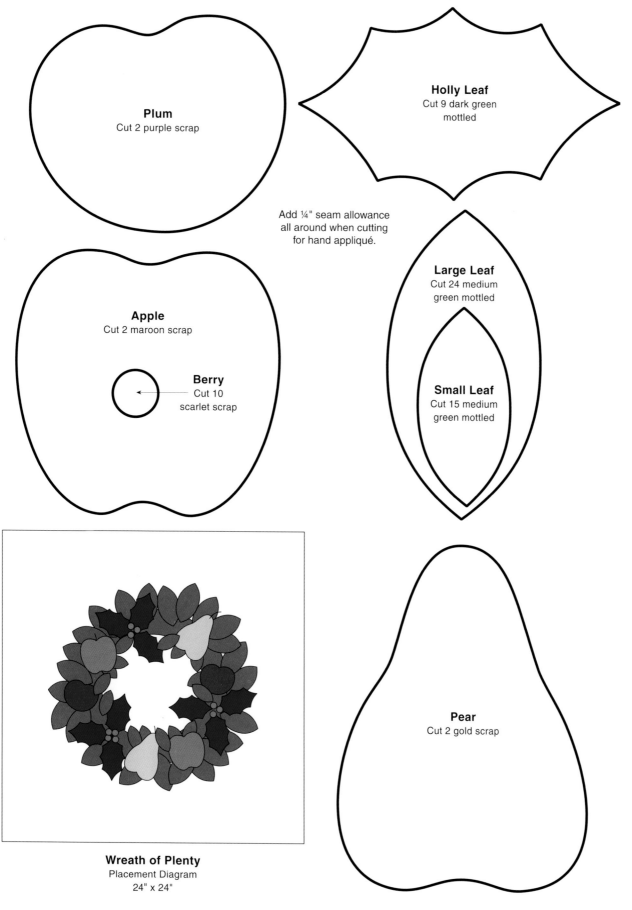

Wreath of Plenty
Placement Diagram
24" x 24"

Pear
Cut 2 gold scrap

Vintage Patchwork Stocking

Have an old-fashioned Christmas with a Victorian flare
with crazy-patchwork and vintage fabrics.

Project Specifications
Skill Level: Beginner
Stocking Size: 19" long

Materials
- 1 dozen large scraps of Dupioni silk, lightweight upholstery fabrics and velvet
- ⅓ yard thin muslin
- ½ yard green velvet for lining
- ½ yard red print velveteen for stocking back and cuff
- Neutral color all-purpose thread
- Variety of colors of 6-strand embroidery floss
- Buttons, beads, lace and other embellishments as desired
- ½ yard ⅜"-wide gold-metallic trim
- Basic sewing tools and supplies

Instructions
Step 1. Trace A and B stocking pieces onto the muslin; cut out to make muslin bases. Mark piecing order given on each muslin base.

Step 2. Join three pair of scraps with right sides together on the longest edges; press and set aside.

Step 3. Place a silk scrap right side up on the unmarked side of the muslin A piece in the piece 1 position; hold up to a light source to check positioning. Check that the scrap

extends at least ¼" beyond the area marked for piece 1 as shown in Figure 1; pin in place.

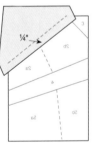

Figure 1
Extend pieces at least
¼" beyond marked
stitching line.

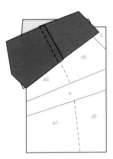

Figure 2
Seam between
pieces matches lines
on muslin base.

Step 4. Select one of the stitched scrap pairs; position it right side down on piece 1 so it extends at least ¼" beyond the area marked for pieces 2a and 2b and that the seam between the 2a and 2b pieces falls roughly where it does on the marked muslin as shown in Figure 2. Pin in place.

Step 5. On the marked side of the muslin, stitch on the marked line between pieces 1 and 2 as shown in Figure 3; flip so the unmarked side is up to check the sewing. Flip pieces back to trim excess seam allowance to ¼", again referring to Figure 3. Press pieces flat and continue to add

pieces in this manner until the muslin A base is covered. Trim excess at edges to match muslin base.

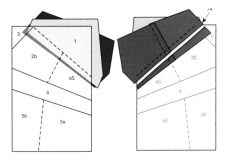

Figure 3
Stitch on marked 1-2 line;
trim seam allowance to ¼".

Step 6. Complete the B section as for A.

Step 7. Sew A to B edges as shown in Figure 4; press seam toward A.

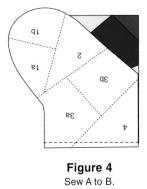

Figure 4
Sew A to B.

Step 8. Using 3 strands of embroidery floss in colors of choice, create rows of embroidery stitches along seam lines. **Note:** *Refer to page 175 for a variety of stitch choices.*

Step 9. Add buttons, lace, beads or other embellishments as desired.

Step 10. Place the stitched stocking right sides together with the red print velveteen and cut a stocking back. Repeat to cut two lining pieces from green velvet.

Step 11. Join the stocking front and back with right sides together, leaving top edge open; repeat with lining pieces.

Step 12. Turn the patchwork stocking right side out; place the stocking lining inside with wrong side of lining against the muslin base.

Step 13. Machine-baste top edges of stocking and lining together.

Step 14. Cut a 5" x 12½" strip red print velveteen for cuff. Join on short ends to make a tube.

Step 15. Place tube right sides together around top of stocking. Pin top raw edge of cuff to the raw edge of the stocking opening; stitch all around. Fold remaining raw edge of cuff ¼" to the wrong side.

Step 16. Turn cuff to inside and hand-stitch in place to cover seam between cuff and stocking/lining pieces.

Step 17. Cut a 5" length of gold-metallic trim; fold in half and pin to the inside edge of the stocking on the heel side to make a hanging loop.

Step 18. Sew the remainder of the gold-metallic trim around the cuff ½" from top edge, catching the gold trim loop in the stitching to finish. ❄

Vintage Patchwork Stocking
Placement Diagram
19" long

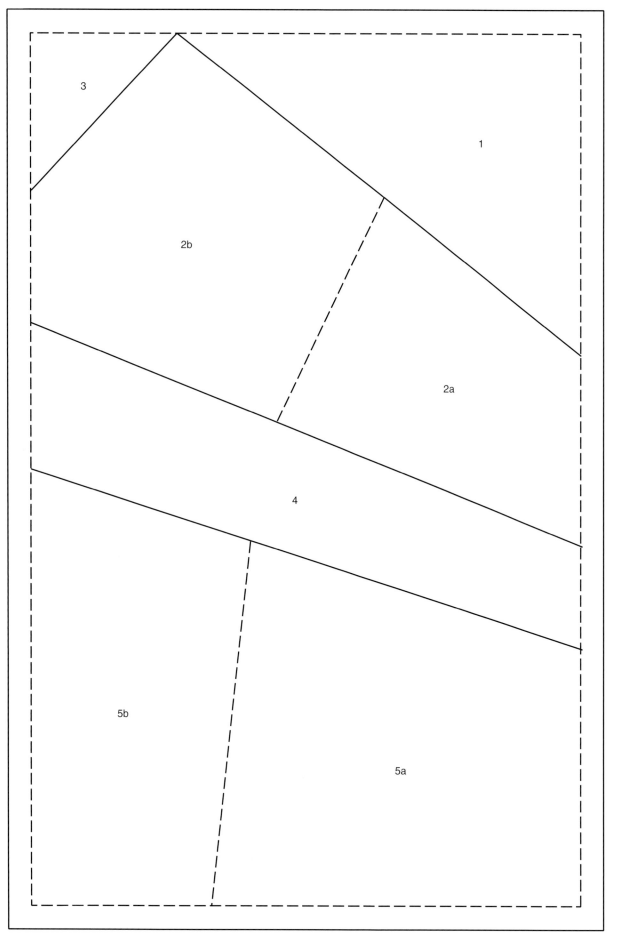

A Base
Cut 1 muslin

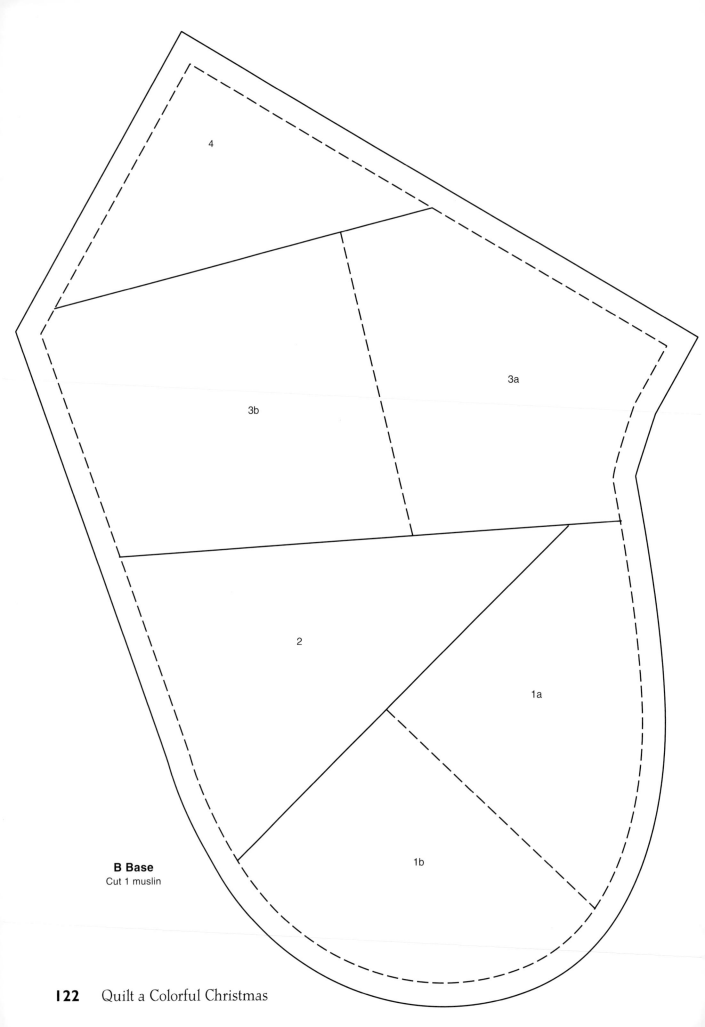

B Base
Cut 1 muslin

4

3b

3a

2

1a

1b

Fancy Holly Table Runner

Bound scalloped border pieces combined with appliquéd borders make a fancy runner out of four easy blocks.

Project Specifications
Skill Level: Advanced
Runner Size: 32½" x 14½" including scallop borders
Block Size: 6" x 6"
Number of Blocks: 4

Materials
- Scrap red solid
- ¼ yard green tonal
- ⅓ yard dark green solid
- ½ yard red tonal
- ⅝ yard white solid
- ¼ yard thin white batting
- Backing 30½" x 12½"
- Batting 30½" x 12½"
- All-purpose thread to match fabrics
- Quilting thread
- Clear nylon monofilament
- ¼ yard fusible web
- ¼" bias bar
- Spray starch and small brush
- Fray preventative (optional)
- Basic sewing tools and supplies and cardboard

Cutting
Step 1. Cut eight 1" x 12" bias strips from the dark green solid for border stems.

Step 2. Cut one strip each red tonal (A), dark green solid (B) and green tonal (C) and two strips white solid (D) 2" by fabric width; subcut strips into 2" square segments.

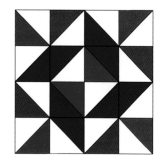

Spinning Triangles
6" x 6" Block

You will need 12 A, 16 B, eight C and 28 D squares. Draw a line from corner to corner on the wrong side of each D square and four A squares.

Step 3. Cut two 1¼" x 24½" E strips and two 1¼" x 8" F strips red tonal.

Step 4. Cut two 2¾" x 26" G strips and two 2¾" x 12½" H strips white solid.

Step 5. Prepare template for I scallop piece; cut as directed on the pattern.

Step 6. Bond the fusible web to the wrong side of the remaining green tonal. Prepare template for leaf shape; trace 48 leaf shapes onto the paper side of the fusible web. Cut out shapes on traced lines; remove paper backing. Apply fray preventative to edges, if desired.

Step 7. Trace the berry pattern onto cardboard; repeat for five or more cardboard shapes. Cut 48 berries from red solid, adding a ¼" seam allowance all around.

Step 8. Cut (42) 2" x 5" J bias strips red tonal.

Piecing the Blocks

Step 1. To piece the blocks, place an unmarked A square right sides together with a D square. Referring to Figure 1, sew ¼" on each side of the drawn line on D; cut apart on the drawn line and press seam toward A to complete two A-D units. Repeat to make 16 A-D units.

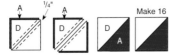

Figure 1
Sew ¼" on each side of the drawn line on A; cut apart on the drawn line to complete 2 A-D units.

Step 2. Repeat Step 1 with A and B to make eight A-B units, with B and D to make 24 B-D units and with C and D to make 16 C-D units referring to Figure 2.

Figure 2
Make A-B, B-D and C-D units.

Step 3. Arrange the units in four rows with four units each as shown in Figure 3; join units in rows. Press seams in adjacent rows in opposite directions. Join the rows to complete one block; repeat for four blocks. Press seams in one direction.

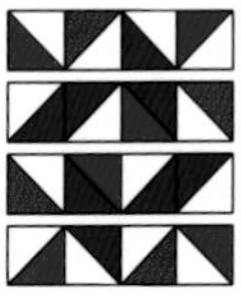

Figure 3
Arrange the units in 4 rows with 4 units each.

Completing the Top

Step 1. Join the blocks to complete the pieced center referring to Figure 4; press seams in one direction.

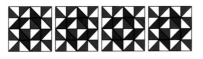

Figure 4
Join the blocks to complete the pieced center.

Step 2. Sew an E strip to opposite long sides and an F strip to each short end of the pieced center; press seams toward E and F.

Step 3. Sew a G strip to opposite long sides and an H strip to each short end of the pieced center; press seams toward E and F strips.

Step 4. Fold the 1" x 12" bias stem strips in half along length with wrong sides together; stitch along long raw edges using a ¼" seam allowance to make a tube as shown in Figure 5.

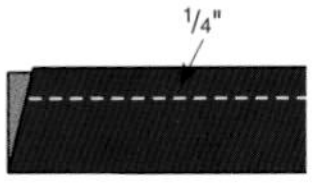

Figure 5
Stitch along long raw edges using a ¼" seam allowance to make a tube.

Figure 6
Insert the ¼" bias bar into the tube and roll the seam to the center back.

Step 5. Trim the seam allowance to ⅛" from stitching line. Insert the ¼" bias bar into the tube and roll the seam to the center back as shown in Figure 6; press on both sides. Let cool, remove bias bar and press the right side of each stem strip again.

Step 6. Arrange and pin three stem strips onto each G strip and one stem strip on each H strip using the stem placement pattern as a guide. **Note:** *Ends of stem strips are butted under berries on sides and at corners.* Trim away excess strip at butted ends.

Step 7. Hand-stitch the stem strips in place.

Step 8. Using a knotted double thread, baste ⅛" from edge of a berry circle; place a cardboard circle in the center of the berry shape and pull the thread to gather the fabric around the cardboard circle as shown in Figure 7.

Figure 7
Baste ⅛" from edge of a berry circle; place a cardboard circle in the center of the berry shape and pull the thread to gather the fabric around the cardboard circle.

Step 9. Spray some of the spray starch into the cover of the can and, using the small brush, apply spray starch to edges of the gathered berry; press. Turn over and spray starch to the right side. Let dry; clip thread. Remove cardboard circle; press again. Repeat for 18 berries.

Step 10. Arrange and fuse holly leaves on the stitched stem with a leaf in each corner, five on each H strip and 17 on each G strip referring to the stem placement pattern and the Placement Diagram.

Step 11. Referring to the stem placement pattern and the Placement Diagram, pin a berry to the base of each corner leaf, two on each H strip and five on each G strip, covering the ends of the stem strips on G.

Step 12. Using clear nylon monofilament and a machine blindstitch, stitch around each leaf and berry to secure.

Making Scallop Pieces

Step 1. Sandwich and pin an I batting piece between the wrong sides of two I pieces.

Step 2. Fold a J strip with wrong sides together along length; press.

Step 3. Pin and stitch a J strip to the curved edges of the layered I pieces as shown in Figure 8. Fold J over the stitched seam; topstitch in place with matching all-purpose thread as shown in Figure 9. Trim excess at ends, again referring to Figure 9. Repeat for 42 I-J units.

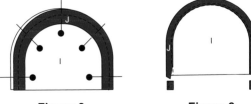

Figure 8
Pin and stitch a J strip to the curved edges of the layered I pieces.

Figure 9
Fold J over the stitched seam; topstitch in place; trim excess at ends.

Step 4. Pin six I-J units to the right side of each H strip, starting ¼" from each corner, overlapping as necessary as shown in Figure 10; baste to hold in place. Repeat with 15 I-J units on each G strip.

Figure 10
Pin 6 I-J units on H, starting ¼" from corner.

Figure 11
Pin the backing piece to the right side of the completed top with I-J units tucked inside.

Finishing the Quilt

Step 1. Pin the backing piece to the right side of the completed top with I-J units tucked inside as shown in Figure 11.

Step 2. Pin the batting piece to the wrong side of the layered top. Stitch all around through all layers, leaving a 10" opening on one side. Reinforce corners and beginning and end with backstitching.

Step 3. Trim corners; turn right side out through the opening. Press edges to make flat; press seam of opening edges inside ¼". Hand-stitch opening closed; press.

Step 4. Hand- or machine-quilt as desired to finish. ❄

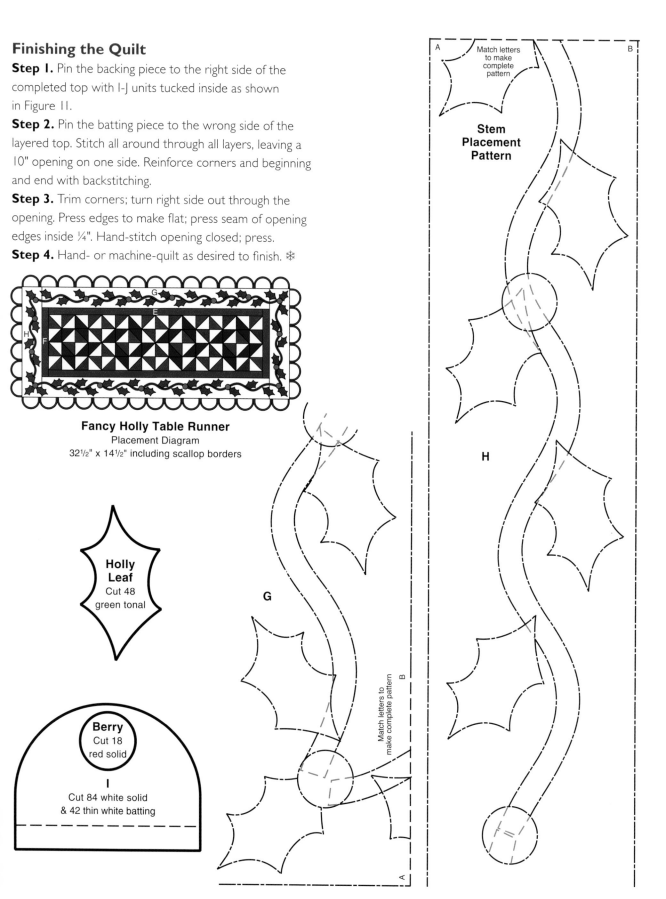

Fancy Holly Table Runner
Placement Diagram
32½" x 14½" including scallop borders

Holly Leaf
Cut 48
green tonal

Berry
Cut 18
red solid

I
Cut 84 white solid
& 42 thin white batting

Stem Placement Pattern

A — Match letters to make complete pattern — B

H

G

B

Match letters to make complete pattern

A

Holly, Wood & Vine

A combination of holly and vine prints inspired the unique name of this delightful bed-size quilt.

Project Specifications

Skill Level: Intermediate
Quilt Size: 90" x 106"
Block Size: 15" x 15"
Number of Blocks: 20

Materials

- ⅓ yard each 2 different green prints
- ½ yard red tonal
- ⅔ yard each 4 different red prints
- 1¾ yards small black floral
- 1⅞ yards black print
- 3⅜ yards cream tonal
- 3⅛ yards large black floral
- Backing 96" x 112"
- Batting 96" x 112"
- Neutral color all-purpose thread
- Quilting thread
- Basic sewing tools and supplies

Cutting

Step 1. Cut two 4½" by fabric width strips from each green print; subcut strips into (10) 4½" A squares each fabric.

Step 2. Cut (10) 2½" by fabric width strips small black floral; subcut strips into (160) 2½" B squares. Draw a line from corner to corner on each B square.

Step 3. Cut (15) 2½" by fabric width strips cream tonal; subcut strips into (240) 2½" C squares.

Step 4. Cut four 2½" by fabric width strips from each

Holly Stars
15" x 15" Block

red print; subcut two strips of each fabric into (40) 1½" D rectangles. Subcut the remaining two strips of each fabric into (20) 2½" E squares.

Step 5. Cut two 8½" by fabric width strips black print; subcut strips into (40) 1½" F strips.

Step 6. Cut two 10½" by fabric width strips black print; subcut strips into (40) 1½" G strips.

Step 7. Cut (12) 2⅞" by fabric width strips cream tonal; subcut strips into (160) 2⅞" H squares. Draw a line from corner to corner on each H square.

Step 8. Cut three 2⅞" by fabric width strips from each red print; subcut strips into (40) 2⅞" I squares each fabric.

Step 9. Cut one 14½" by fabric width strip cream tonal; subcut strip into (40) 1" J strips.

Step 10. Cut one 15½" by fabric width strip cream tonal; subcut strip into (40) 1" K strips.

Step 11. Cut one 15½" by fabric width strip small black floral; subcut strip into (25) 1½" L sashing strips.

Step 12. Cut (10) 1½" by fabric width strips small black floral; join strips on short ends to make one long strip. Subcut strip into six 65½" M sashing strips.

Step 13. Cut eight 1" by fabric width strips cream tonal; join strips on short ends to make one long strip. Subcut strip into two 81½" N strips and two 66½" O strips.

Step 14. Cut eight 1½" by fabric width strips red tonal; join strips on short ends to make one long strip. Subcut strip into two 82½" P strips and two 68½" Q strips.

Step 15. Cut nine 11½" by fabric width strips large black floral; join strips on short ends to make one long strip. Subcut strip into two 84½" R strips and two 90½" S strips.

Step 16. Cut (10) 2¼" by fabric width strips black print for binding.

Piecing the Blocks

Step 1. To piece one block, select matching red print D, E and I pieces. Sew D to opposite sides of C as shown in Figure 1; press seams toward D. Repeat for four C-D units.

Figure 1
Sew D to opposite
sides of C.

Figure 2
Sew B to a C-D
unit as shown.

Step 2. Place a B square on the D end of one C-D unit as shown in Figure 2. Stitch on the marked line, trim seam allowance to ¼" and press B to the right side, again referring to Figure 2. Repeat on the opposite end of the C-D unit to complete a B-C-D unit as shown in Figure 3. Repeat for four units.

Figure 3
Complete a B-C-D
unit as shown.

Figure 4
Sew a B-C-D unit to
opposite sides of A.

Step 3. Sew a B-C-D unit to opposite sides of A as shown in Figure 4; press seams toward A.

Step 4. Sew E to each B end of the two remaining B-C-D units as shown in Figure 5; press seams toward E.

Step 5. Sew a B-C-D-E unit to opposite sides of the A-B-C-D unit as shown in Figure 6 to complete the block center; press seams toward A-B-C-D.

Figure 5
Sew E to each B end of the
2 remaining B-C-D units.

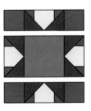

Figure 6
Sew a B-C-D-E unit to opposite
sides of the A-B-C-D unit.

Step 6. Sew F to opposite sides and G to the top and bottom of the block center; press seams toward F and G.

Step 7. Place an H square right sides together with an I square; stitch ¼" on each side of the marked line as shown in Figure 7. Cut apart on the marked line to complete two H-I units, again referring to Figure 7. Repeat for 16 H-I units.

Figure 7
Complete H-I units as shown.

Step 8. Join four H-I units with C as shown in Figure 8; repeat for four units. Press seams toward C.

Figure 8
Join 4 H-I units with C.

Step 9. Sew a C-H-I unit to the F sides of the pieced center as shown in Figure 9; press seams toward F.

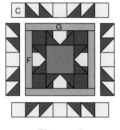

Figure 9
Join units as shown.

Step 10. Sew a C square to each end of the remaining two C-H-I units; press seams toward C. Sew these units to the remaining sides of the pieced center, again referring to Figure 9; press seams toward G strips.

Step 11. Sew J to opposite sides and K to the top and bottom of the pieced unit to complete one block as shown in Figure 10; press seams toward J and K. Repeat for 20 blocks, five of each fabric combination.

Figure 10
Sew J and K to the pieced
unit to complete 1 block.

Completing the Top

Step 1. Arrange the blocks in five rows of four blocks each with one of each combination in each row, placing blocks of different fabrics in a pleasing arrangement. Join the blocks with five L strips to make a row; press seams toward L. Repeat for five rows.

Step 2. Join the rows with six M strips, beginning and ending with a strip; press seams toward M.

Step 3. Sew an N strip to opposite long sides and O strips to the top and bottom of the pieced center; press seams toward N and O.

Step 4. Sew a P strip to opposite long sides and Q strips to the top and bottom of the pieced center; press seams toward P and Q.

Step 5. Sew an R strip to opposite long sides and S strips to the top and bottom of the pieced center; press seams toward R and S to complete the top.

Finishing the Quilt

Step 1. Sandwich batting between the completed top and prepared backing; pin or baste to hold layers together.

Step 2. Quilt as desired by hand or machine; remove basting or pins.

Step 3. When quilting is complete, trim batting and backing even with quilt top.

Step 4. Join the binding strips on short ends to make one long strip. Fold the strip in half along length with wrong sides together; press.

Step 5. Sew binding to quilt edges, mitering corners and overlapping ends. Fold binding to the back side and stitch in place. ❄

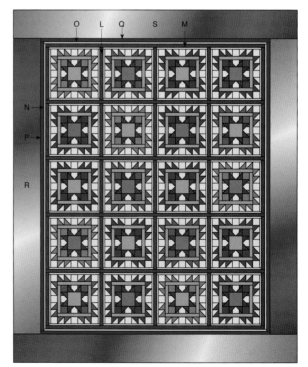

Holly, Wood & Vine
Placement Diagram
90" x 106"

Reindeer Tracks

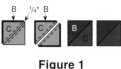

Sashing squares combine with block corners to create a secondary design in this little quilt.

Project Specifications

Skill Level: Beginner
Quilt Size: 23½" x 23½"
Block Size: 4" x 4"
Number of Blocks: 16

Materials

- ⅓ yard medium green print
- ⅓ yard cream tonal
- ½ yard each red and dark green prints
- Backing 28" x 28"
- Batting 28" x 28"
- All-purpose thread to match fabrics
- Quilting thread
- Basic sewing tools and supplies

Cutting

Step 1. Cut three 1½" by fabric width strips cream tonal; subcut into (72) 1½" A squares.

Step 2. Cut two 1⅞" by fabric width strips each dark green (B) and red (C) prints; subcut strips into (36) 1⅞" squares each B and C. Draw a line from corner to corner on the wrong side of each C square.

Step 3. Cut three 2½" by fabric width strips medium green print; subcut strips into (64) 1½" D pieces.

Step 4. Cut one 4½" by fabric width strip red print; subcut into (40) 1" E strips.

Step 5. Cut one 1" by fabric width strip dark green print; subcut into (21) 1" F squares.

Step 6. Cut one 1½" by fabric width strip dark green

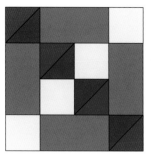

Reindeer Tracks
4" x 4" Block

print; subcut into four 3½" H pieces and four 2½" G pieces.

Step 7. Cut four 1" x 18" I strips cream tonal.

Step 8. Cut four 2½" x 18" J strips dark green print.

Step 9. Cut three 2¼" by fabric width strips red print for binding.

Piecing the Blocks

Step 1. To piece a B-C unit, referring to Figure 1, place B right sides together with C; stitch ¼" on each side of the marked line. Cut apart on the marked line; press seam to one side on each unit. Repeat to make 72 B-C units.

Figure 1
Make B-C units as shown.

Step 2. Referring to Figure 2 to piece one block, join two B-C units with two A squares; press seams toward A. Join two A-B-C units; press seam in one direction. Add D to opposite sides of the pieced unit; press seams toward D.

Step 3. Sew a B-C unit to one end and an A square to the other end of D; press seams toward D. Repeat for two units.

Step 4. Sew a B-C-D-A unit to opposite sides of the pieced center unit to complete one block; press seams toward B-C-D-A units.

Step 5. Repeat Steps 2–4 to complete 16 blocks.

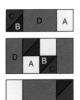

Figure 2
Join units to
complete 1 block.

Completing the Top

Step 1. Join four blocks with three E strips to make a block row as shown in Figure 3; press seams toward E. Repeat for four rows.

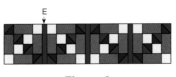

Figure 3
Join 4 blocks with 3 E
strips to make a block row.

Step 2. Join four E strips with three F squares to make a sashing row as shown in Figure 4; repeat for seven sashing rows. Press seams toward E.

Figure 4
Join 4 E strips with 3 F squares
to make a sashing row.

Step 3. Join the block rows with three sashing rows as shown in Figure 5; press seams toward sashing rows.

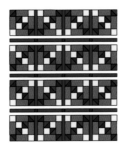

Figure 5
Join the block rows
with 3 sashing rows.

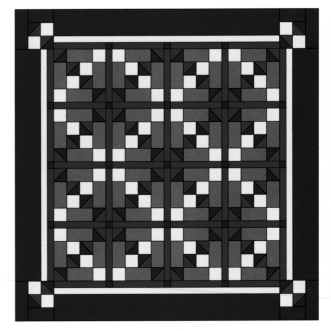

Reindeer Tracks
Placement Diagram
23¹⁄₂" x 23¹⁄₂"

Step 4. Sew a sashing row to an I strip to a J strip to make a border strip as shown in Figure 6; press seams toward I and J. Repeat for four border strips.

Figure 6
Sew a sashing row to an
I strip to a J strip.

Step 5. Join two B-C units with two A squares and add G and H to make a corner unit as shown in Figure 7; press seams toward A, then in one direction, then toward G and H. Repeat for four units.

Figure 7
Make a corner
unit as shown.

Step 6. Referring to Figure 8, sew a border strip to the top and bottom of the pieced center; press seams toward strips.

Figure 8
Sew a border strip to
the top and bottom of
the pieced center.

Figure 9
Add a corner unit to each end
of the remaining border strips.

Step 7. Add a corner unit to each end of the remaining border strips as shown in Figure 9; press seams away from corner units. Sew a strip to the remaining sides to complete the pieced top referring to the Placement Diagram; press seams toward strips.

Finishing the Quilt

Step 1. Sandwich batting between the completed top and prepared backing; pin or baste to hold layers together.

Step 2. Quilt as desired by hand or machine; remove pins or basting.

Step 3. When quilting is complete, trim batting and backing even with quilt top.

Step 4. Join the binding strips on short ends to make one long strip. Fold the strip in half along length with wrong sides together; press.

Step 5. Sew binding to quilt edges, mitering corners and overlapping ends. Fold binding to the backside and stitch in place. ❄

DESIGN BY **BARBARA A. CLAYTON**

Friendly Snowman Tree Skirt

A friendly snowman reminds us of the cold of winter in this lovable appliquéd tree skirt.

Project Specifications

Skill Level: Advanced

Tree Skirt Size: 42½" diameter without prairie points

Materials

- Scraps, orange, yellow, gold, light and medium blue and light and dark red prints, tonals or mottleds
- Scraps black solid and black tonal
- Scrap brown mottled
- ¼ yard light blue print
- ¼ yard each 2 medium and one dark green prints, tonals or mottleds
- ½ yard white solid
- 1⅓ yards white tonal
- 2⅝ yards 45"-wide blue snowflake print
- Batting 44" x 44"
- All-purpose thread to match fabrics
- Clear nylon monofilament
- White quilting thread
- 2 yards fusible web
- Non-stick appliqué pressing sheet
- Fray preventative (optional)
- Basic sewing tools and supplies, water-erasable marker, pencil, string, 43" square newsprint and narrow masking tape

Cutting & Assembling the Tree Skirt Top

Step 1. Tie a string around a pencil; cut long end of string to 21½". Hold the string in the center of the square of newsprint and draw a 43" circle as shown in Figure 1; cut out to make tree skirt pattern.

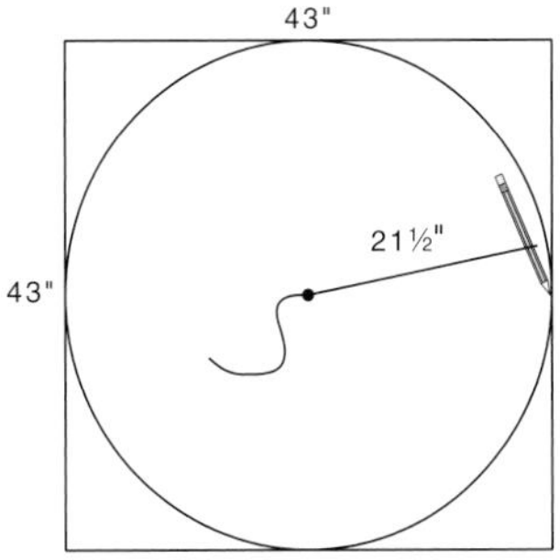

Figure 1
Draw a 43" circle as shown.

Step 2. Fold the paper pattern to divide into eight equal parts as shown in Figure 2.

Figure 2
Fold the paper pattern to divide into 8 equal parts.

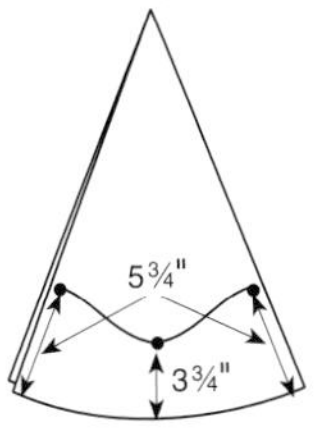

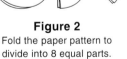

Figure 3
Mark pattern as shown.

Step 3. Referring to Figure 3, measure up from the bottom on both folded edges and mark at 5¾". Find the center of the curved edges; measure up 3¾". Draw a sloping curve from the 5¾" point down to the 3¾" point and up to the second 5¾"point to create the snow pattern line. Repeat all around.

Step 4. Using the unfolded pattern, cut one tree skirt top; cut a backing piece ½" larger all around from the blue

snowflake print. Draw a 4" circle in the center of the tree skirt top; cut out. Fold the fabric circle into four equal parts; cut from the edge of the cut circle to the outside edge along one fold line to make tree skirt opening.

Step 5. Cut the paper pattern along the snowline to make snow pattern; cut one white tonal as shown in Figure 4.

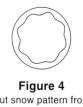

Figure 4
Cut snow pattern from
fabric as shown.

Step 6. Cut (78) 3" × 3" squares from the remaining white tonal, using leftover in the center from cutting snow pattern and remainder of fabric; set aside squares to make prairie points.

Step 7. Place the snow piece right side up on the right side of the tree skirt top; pin edges together. Cut the slit in

the same place on the snow piece. Fold the curved edge of the snow line under ¼" and using a machine blind-hem stitch and clear nylon monofilament, stitch in place.

Step 8. Trim away the excess blue snowflake print from behind the snow to match the ¼" seam of the snow fabric. Fold and crease the tree-skirt top in eighths as in Step 2; set aside.

Appliqué

Step 1. Cut a 12" × 22" piece of fusible web; press onto the wrong side of the white solid; cut around the fused rectangle. Remove paper backing; fuse to the wrong side of the remaining white solid to make a double layer of fabric. **Note:** *This is to keep the fabrics under the snowman shapes from showing through.*

Step 2. Trace appliqué shapes onto the paper side of the fusible web referring to patterns for number of each shape to cut.

Note: *Pieces are given in reverse for fusible appliqué.*

Step 3. Cut out shapes, leaving a margin around each one; fuse shapes to the wrong side of fabric scraps as directed on each piece for color. Cut out shapes on traced lines. Remove paper backing. Transfer detail lines to fabric pieces using a water-erasable marker or pencil. **Note:** *The snowman, hat and tree shapes are cut as complete pieces; the shadow pieces are placed on top with outer edges matching.*

Step 4. Using the non-stick appliqué pressing sheet as the base, layer the pieces on top of the sheet in numerical order, referring to pattern lines for placement. When satisfied with placement; fuse shapes in place. Let cool; remove from pressing sheet. Repeat to build three each snowman and large tree motifs and six small tree motifs.

Step 5. Referring to Figure 5, place one fused snowman motif directly opposite the cut opening and one at each quarter fold mark 3¼" from the bottom edge; fuse in place.

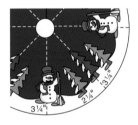

Figure 5
Place motifs as shown.

Step 6. Place a set of one large and two small trees on the eighth marks in between the snowmen and on each side of the back opening with the large tree in the center 3¼" from bottom edge and small trees 2¼" up from bottom edge, again referring to Figure 5.

Step 7. Blind-hem-stitch around each shape using clear nylon monofilment. Satin-stitch eyes on marked lines using black thread.

Making Prairie Points

Step 1. Fold each of the 3" x 3" squares white tonal in half on the diagonal, then in half again to form a prairie point triangle as shown in Figure 6; press and pin to hold. Repeat for 78 prairie points.

Figure 6
Fold square to make prairie points.

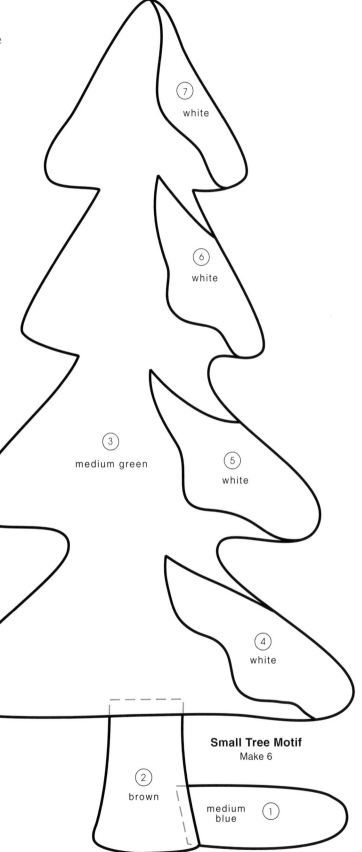

⑦ white

⑥ white

③ medium green

⑤ white

④ white

Small Tree Motif
Make 6

② brown

① medium blue

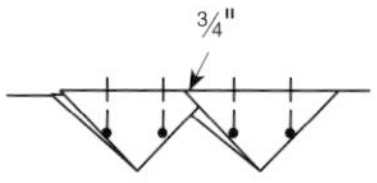

Step 2. Pin the raw edge of the prairie points to the curved edge of the fused top, overlapping about ¾" as shown in Figure 7; adjust to fit. Machine-baste in place to secure, being careful not to stretch the curved edges as you stitch.

¾"

Figure 7
Pin to edge, overlapping ¾'

Finishing the Quilt

Step 1. Lay the batting square on a flat surface; place the backing piece right side up on the batting and pin to hold.

Step 2. Pin the appliquéd top right sides together with the pinned backing/batting layers. Stitch all around, leaving a 10" opening along one straight side of the back skirt opening. Cut the back slit in the backing and batting layers. Clip the corners; trim batting and backing even with the top.

Step 3. Turn the tree skirt right side out through the opening; press opening seam under ¼". Hand-stitch opening closed. Press flat, pulling prairie points out as you press.

Step 4. Pin or baste layers together to hold flat.

Step 5. Using white quilting thread, quilt ¼" from stitched edges all around. Place a long piece of masking tape from the center to the outside edge along the eighth marks; hand-quilt on these lines. Place another piece of tape between each of the quilted lines; hand-quilt on these lines to finish. ❄

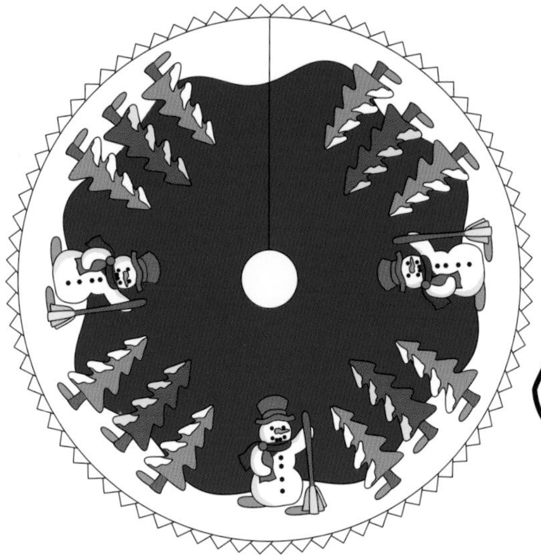

Friendly Snowman Tree Skirt
Placement Diagram
42½" Diameter (without prairie points)

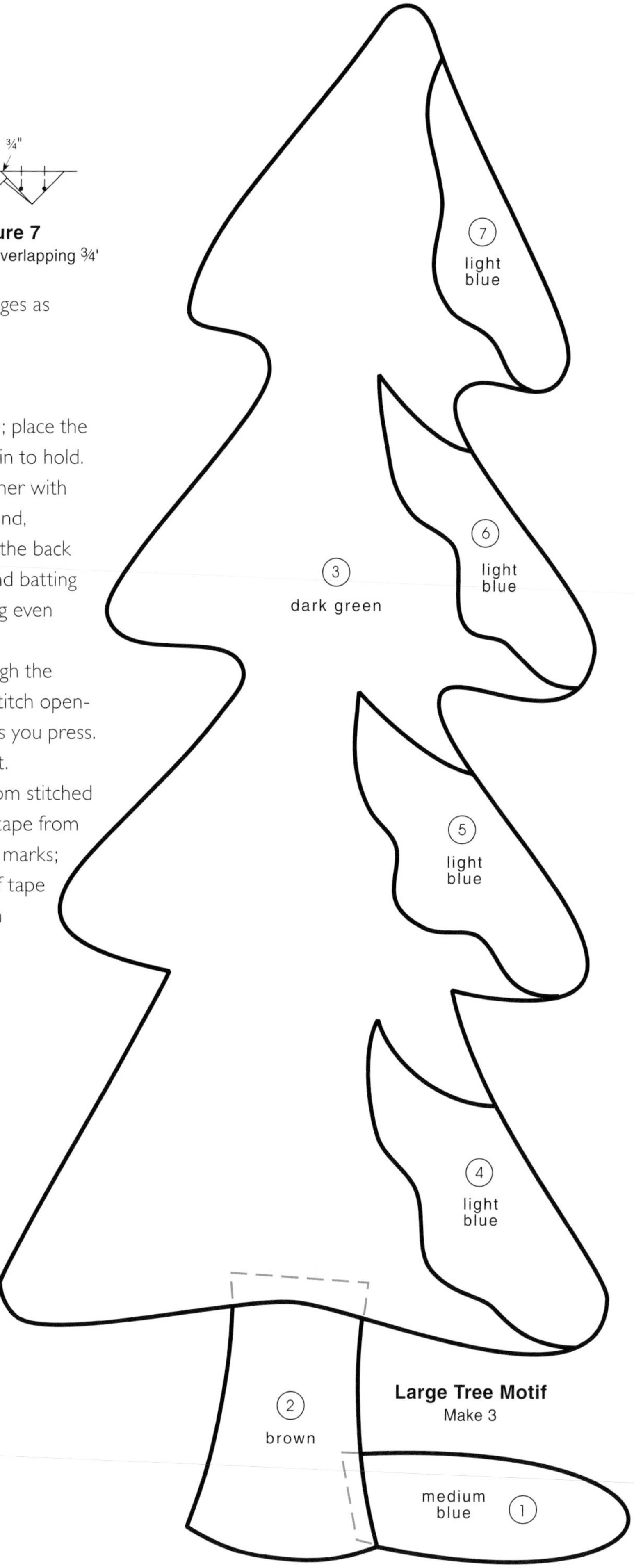

⑦ light blue

③ dark green

⑥ light blue

⑤ light blue

④ light blue

② brown

Large Tree Motif
Make 3

medium blue ①

Friendly Snowman Tree Skirt

Snowman Motif
Make 3

Crazy Christmas Tree

Play with your machine's fancy stitches while you whip up this charming wall quilt.

Project Specifications
Skill Level: Beginner
Quilt Size: 18" x 21"

Materials
- Scrap brown tonal
- Assorted scraps green Christmas prints
- ½ yard red print
- ½ yard cream print
- Backing 22" x 25"
- Batting 22" x 25"
- All-purpose thread to match fabrics
- Gold metallic thread
- ¼ yard double-stick fusible web
- Basic sewing tools and supplies

Cutting
Step 1. Cut one 12½" x 15½" rectangle cream print for A center background; fold and crease to mark the center.

Step 2. Cut one 4¼" by fabric width strip each red and cream prints; subcut the red print strip into six 4¼" B squares and the cream print strip into five 4¼" C squares. Cut each square in half on both diagonals to make 22 B and 18 C triangles; set aside remaining B and C triangles for another project.

Step 3. Cut two 2⅜" x 2⅜" squares each red (D) and cream E prints; cut each square on one diagonal to make four each D and E triangles.

Step 4. Cut three 2¼" by fabric width strips red print for binding.

Completing the Appliquéd Center
Step 1. Draw the tree shape given onto one paper side of the fusible web; remove paper from the remaining side.

Step 2. Cut small pieces of the green scraps and lay on the sticky side of the fusible-web tree, trying not to overlap pieces more than ¼". When the tree shape is complete covered, bond fabrics to the fusible-web shape. **Note:** *You may use the lines on the tree pattern as guides to cut shapes, if desired. Pieces are given in reverse for fusible appliqué.*

Step 3. Turn the tree shape over; cut out along marked lines on the remaining paper side.

Step 4. Repeat with tree trunk shape and brown scrap.

Step 5. Center the tree and trunk shapes on A 2½" from bottom edge using crease lines as guides for placement and slipping the tree trunk under the tree shape ¼" on bottom edge of tree; fuse in place.

Completing the Top
Step 1. Make 22 copies of the F crazy-patch square pattern. Be sure you can see the lines on the wrong side of the pattern.

Step 2. Cut scraps in shapes given on pattern adding at least ¼" all around. **Note:** *Scraps can be any size as long as they fill the entire numbered space with ⅛"–¼" extra for seam allowance.*

Step 3. Referring to Figure 1, place piece 1 on the unmarked side of one F square covering the marked space for piece 1; place piece 2 right sides together with piece 1. Turn paper over; stitch on the line between pieces 1 and 2, extending stitching to outer edge of square and a stitch or two into piece 3.

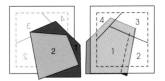

Figure 1
Sew piece 2 to piece 1 on the
marked side of the paper pattern.

Step 4. Referring to Figure 2, turn paper over and trim
seam to ⅛"; press piece 2 to the right side. Continue adding

pieces in this manner until the square is covered; trim edges
even with paper pattern. Repeat for 22 F squares.

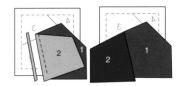

Figure 2
Trim seam; press piece
2 to the right side.

Step 5. Sew B to opposite sides of F and add D to make
a corner unit as shown in Figure 3; press seams toward B
and D. Repeat for four units; remove paper backing from F.

Figure 3
Sew B to opposite
sides of F and add D
to make a corner unit.

Step 6. Sew C and E to F to make an end unit as shown
in Figure 4; repeat for two end units. Press seams toward
C and E; remove paper backing from F.

Figure 4
Sew C and E to F to
make an end unit.

Figure 5
Sew 2 C pieces to F.

Step 7. Sew two C pieces to F as shown in Figure 5;
repeat for two units. Press seams toward C; remove
paper backing from F.

Step 8. Sew B and E to F as shown in Figure 6; repeat
for two units. Press seams toward B and E; remove paper
backing from F.

Figure 6
Sew B and E to F.

Figure 7
Sew B and C to
opposite sides of F.

Step 9. Sew B and C to opposite sides of F as shown in Figure 7; repeat for 12 units. Press seams toward B and C; remove paper backing from F.

Step 10. Join the units as shown in Figure 8 to make two side and two end strips; press seams in one direction.

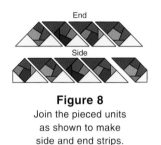

Figure 8
Join the pieced units
as shown to make
side and end strips.

Step 11. Referring to Figure 9, sew the side strips to opposite long sides and end units to opposite short ends of the appliquéd center; add B-D-F corner units to complete the pieced top.

Figure 9
Sew side and end strips
to the center; add B-D-F
corner units.

Finishing the Quilt

Step 1. Sandwich batting between the completed top and prepared backing; pin or baste to hold layers together.

Step 2. Quilt as desired by hand or machine; remove pins or basting.

Step 3. Using gold metallic thread and decorative machine stitches, stitch along seams of the crazy-patch tree and F squares.

Step 4. When quilting and decorative stitching is complete, trim batting and backing even with quilt top.

Step 5. Join the binding strips on short ends to make one long strip. Fold the strip in half along length with wrong sides together; press.

Step 6. Sew binding to quilt edges, mitering corners and overlapping ends. Fold binding to the back side and stitch in place. ❄

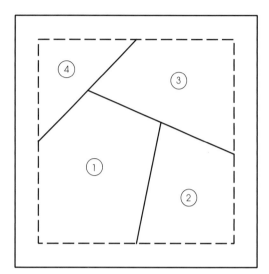

F Crazy-Patch Square
Make 22 copies

Crazy Christmas Tree
Placement Diagram
18" x 21"

Crazy Christmas Tree

Tree
Cut pieces from
assorted green
Christmas prints

Trunk
Cut 1 brown

Quilter's Ornaments

A quilter's Christmas tree should be filled with quilted ornaments.

Golden Ball

Project Specifications

Skill Level: Beginner

Ornament Size: 4¼" x 4⅛"

Materials

- 3 coordinating scraps gold/ivory check, ivory tonal and green metallic
- Scrap muslin
- Scrap thin batting
- 8" x 8" square thin batting
- All-purpose thread to match fabrics
- Gold metallic floss
- 41 (3mm) gold seed beads
- 3 (⅝") gold buttons
- 18" (⅞"-wide) gold wire-edge ribbon
- Metallic gold paint pen or metallic gold paint and brush
- 8" piece thin gold cord
- Basic sewing tools and supplies and small beading or quilting needle

Instructions

Note: If making a quantity of ornaments, sew long strips of fabric together and subcut into 5"-square segments.

Step 1. For one ornament, cut two strips 1½" x 5" gold/ivory check (A), two 1" x 5" ivory (B) and one green metallic (C) strip 1½" x 5". Cut one 5" x 5" square thin batting.

Step 2. Join the A, B and C strips with right sides together along the 5" length as shown in Figure 1; press seams away from C.

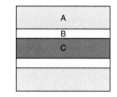

Figure 1
Join A, B and C
strips as shown.

Step 3. Place the pieced rectangle on the batting right side up; baste to hold.

Step 4. Using 1 strand gold metallic floss, center and embroider a small featherstitch along each of the B strips as shown in Figure 2. ***Note:*** *The embroidered area should be centered and about 3¾" long to avoid the seams.*

Figure 2
Make small featherstitches.

Step 5. Using beading or quilting needle, sew a gold seed bead at the tip of every stitch except the beginning and ending stitches on each strip.

Step 6. To make ornament cap, trace around the pattern onto the muslin and fold the muslin in half with traced lines on top; pin to a scrap of thin batting. Stitch from folded edge down each side, leaving open at the bottom edge.

Step 7. Trim corners and batting close to seam; turn right side out. Use paint pen or paint and brush to color cap metallic gold; let dry.

Step 8. Use pattern to cut ornament out of embroidered and pieced top and a back from one of the fabrics.

Step 9. Place cap at center top of ornament front with raw edges aligned; sew all around ornament a scant ¼" from edge, catching end of cap in stitches.

Step 10. With right sides facing, pin backing and top together; sew all around, leaving open at top as indicated on pattern. Clip curves; turn right side out. Fold in seam allowance; slipstitch closed.

Step 11. Center and sew three buttons to C, sewing through all layers.

Step 12. Tie ribbon in a bow; tie a knot at each end of ribbon tail. Tack bow to front of ornament, just below cap. If desired, shape ribbon tails and tack to ornament to secure.

Step 13. Thread needle with gold cord; take a small stitch at top back of cap. Tie ends in a knot for hanger.

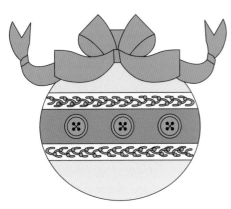

Golden Ball
Placement Diagram
4¼" x 4⅛"

Star

Project Specifications
Skill Level: Beginner
Ornament Size: 4" x 4"

Materials
- 3 coordinating scraps red, gold and green prints
- 4½" x 4½" square batting
- All-purpose thread to match fabrics
- ⅝" green button
- 18" (⅜"-wide) red grosgrain ribbon
- Basic sewing tools and supplies

Instructions

Step 1. Cut (12) 1¼" x 1¼" squares each from red (A) and gold (B) prints.

Step 2. For star points, draw a pencil line from one corner to the opposite corner on the wrong side of eight B squares.

Step 3. Referring to Figure 3, place a B square right sides together with an A square; sew on traced lines. Cut 3/16" from stitch line on one side of seam and open the stitched unit. Finger-press. Repeat for eight A-B units.

Figure 3
Complete A-B units as shown.

Step 4. Arrange the A-B units with the A and B squares in four rows referring to Figure 4; join in rows. Finger-press seams in adjacent rows in opposite directions. Join rows; finger-press seams in one direction.

Figure 4
Arrange A-B units with A and B squares.

Step 5. Cut two 1" x 3½" D strips and two 1" x 4½" E strips green print. Sew D to the top and bottom and E to opposite sides of the pieced center.

Step 6. Cut a 4½" x 4½" square green print. Layer batting, backing right side up and pieced block right side down; pin. Sew all around, leaving a 2" opening on one side.

Step 7. Clip corners; trim batting close to seam. Turn right side out through opening; press. Fold in seam allowance on opening; hand-stitch opening closed.

Step 8. Sew the green button to the center of the ornament through all layers.

Step 9. Quilt as desired by hand or machine.

Step 10. Tie a knot at each end of ribbon; fold ribbon in half and position the ornament over ribbon so ends extend 2" below. Tack ribbon in place on the back of the ornament to finish.

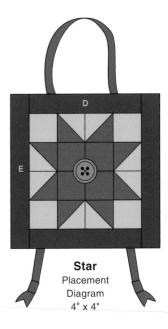

Star
Placement Diagram
4" x 4"

Fun Photo

Project Specifications

Skill Level: Beginner
Ornament Size: 4" x 4¾"; size varies with photo used

Materials

- Sheet of ink-jet printable fabric
- Small pieces of red solid and Christmas print
- Scraps batting and backing fabric
- All-purpose thread to match fabrics
- 6 (⁷⁄₁₆"–⁹⁄₁₆") buttons in various colors
- Christmas novelty button or painted wood cutout
- 20" (⅜"-wide) red grosgrain ribbon
- All-purpose thread to match fabrics
- Inkjet color printer or copier
- Basic sewing tools and supplies

Instructions

Step 1. Print photo onto ink-jet printable fabric following manufacturer's instructions. Trim photo to desired size, including seam allowance.

Step 2. Cut ¾"-wide strips from red fabric to fit sides of photo; sew to sides and press seams toward strips. Repeat to make top and bottom borders.

Step 3. Repeat with 1¼"-wide strips of Christmas print, stitching strips first to sides and then top and bottom. Press seams toward Christmas-print strips.

Step 4. Cut batting and backing fabric the same size as the stitched top.

Step 5. Layer batting, backing right side up and pieced block right side down; pin. Sew all around, leaving a 2" opening on one side.

Step 6. Clip corners; trim batting close to seam. Turn right side out through opening; press. Fold in seam allowance on opening; hand-stitch opening closed.

Step 7. Arrange buttons around one corner, slightly overlapping a few; stitch in place.

Note: *If using a painted wood cutout, drill two small holes, if desired, so cutout can be stitched onto ornament like a button.*

Step 8. Quilt in the ditch of border seams by hand or machine.

Step 9. Tie a knot at each end of ribbon; fold ribbon in half and position ornament over ribbon so ends extend 2" below. Tack ribbon in place on ornament back to finish. ❊

Fun Photo
Placement
Diagram
4" x 4¾"

Golden Ball
Cut 1 from pieced strip
& 1 each backing &
batting

Place cap between 2 center dots
Leave open between 2 outer dots

Cap
Cut 1 each muslin
& batting

Santa Gift Bag

Fill this gift bag with holiday gifts for a special person.

Project Specifications
Skill Level: Beginner
Bag Size: 17½" x 21½"

Materials
- ⅛ yard peach solid
- ⅛ yard white tonal
- ¼ yard red tonal
- ¾ yard Santa print
- 1 yard green print
- Batting 28" x 38"
- All-purpose thread to match fabrics
- Black and red 6-strand embroidery floss
- Basting spray
- Basic sewing tools and supplies

Cutting
Step 1. Cut one 14½" x 35½" rectangle Santa print for A bag bottom. **Note:** *Fabric used in sample was a horizontal stripe print. If using a vertical stripe print, 1¼ yards are needed to complete the sample.*
Step 2. Cut one 2¼" by fabric width strip each red and white tonals and peach solid. Prepare template for B using pattern given. Referring to Figure 1, cut B pieces from strips as directed on pattern for color and number to cut.

Figure 1
Cut B and C
pieces from strips.

Step 3. Cut one 4" by fabric width print C strip. Prepare template C using pattern given. Again referring to Figure 1, cut 10 C pieces from strip.
Step 4. Cut two 1½" x 35½" D strips red tonal.
Step 5. Cut one 2½" x 35½" E strip Santa print.
Step 6. Cut one 3" by fabric width strip green print for handles; remove the selvage edge from each end of the strips. Cut into two equal-length strips.
Step 7. Cut one 24" x 38" piece green print for lining.
Step 8. Cut two 1" x 22" strips batting from the 28" x 38" batting rectangle; set aside remainder of batting for bag.

Piecing the Bag Top
Step 1. Sew a red tonal B to a peach solid B and add a white tonal B to the peach solid sides to complete one Santa unit as shown in Figure 2; repeat for 10 units. Press seams toward darker fabrics.

Figure 2
Complete a Santa
unit as shown.

Step 2. Transfer facial features to the peach solid B piece using pencil and pattern given.
Step 3. Join the 10 Santa units with C to make a strip as shown in Figure 3; press seams toward C.

Figure 3
Join the 10 Santa units with C to make a strip.

Step 4. Center and sew a D strip to opposite long sides of the pieced Santa strip; press seams toward D. **Note:** *The edges of the C pieces will extend beyond edges of D. Trim C even with D strips at ends as shown in Figure 4.*

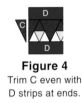

Figure 4
Trim C even with
D strips at ends.

Step 5. Center and sew E to the top edge and A to the bottom edge of the pieced strip; press seams toward A and E to complete the pieced bag top.

Step 6. Apply basting spray to one side of the batting rectangle; layer the pieced bag top on the batting.

Step 7. Using all-purpose thread to match fabrics, stitch in the ditch of seams between D pieces and the pieced Santa strip and as desired on the E section. When quilting is complete, trim batting edges even with the pieced bag top.

Step 8. Using 2 strands of black embroidery floss, make French knots for eyes, wrapping the floss around the needle 3–4 times. Repeat with 2 strands red embroidery floss for nose and use a backstitch for mouth.

Making Handles

Step 1. Fold one long edge of each handle strip ¼" to the wrong side and press.

Step 2. Fold over opposite long edge of each strip 1" as shown in Figure 5 and press; fold the pressed ¼" edge over ¾" on top of the raw edge of the pressed 1" edge and press.

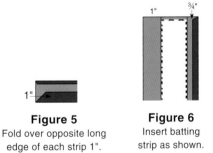

Figure 5
Fold over opposite long
edge of each strip 1".

Figure 6
Insert batting
strip as shown.

Step 3. Open the pressed edges of each strip and insert the 1"-wide batting strip, aligning batting strip with pressing lines as shown in Figure 6.

Step 4. Refold pressed edges over the batting, first folding over the 1" edges and overlapping with the ¾" finished edge; press to make 1"-wide strips.

Step 5. Stitch along folded-over edge along center of strips as shown in Figure 7. Stitch ¼" from each side of the stitched line as shown in Figure 8.

Figure 7
Stitch along
folded-over edge.

Figure 8
Stitch ¼" from each side
of the first stitched line.

Step 6. Square-up ends of each strip to complete handles.

Attaching Handles

Step 1. Fold the quilted bag top in half along the width and lay on a flat surface.

Step 2. Measure in 3¾" from the raw edge and pin the right side of one end of one handle to the top right side edge of the bag as shown in Figure 9. Measure in 3½" from the folded edge and pin the opposite end of the same handle right sides together with bag top edge, again referring to Figure 9. **Note:** *The right side of the handle strip is the side without the overlapped edge.*

Figure 9
Pin handle ends right
sides together with bag
top edge as shown.

Step 3. Turn folded bag top over, align and pin the second handle even with the ends of the handle pinned in Step 2 as shown in Figure 10.

Figure 10
Pin second handle ends
even with ends of first
handle strip.

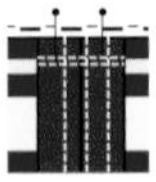

Figure 11
Machine-stitch over ends
of handles several times
to secure in place.

Step 4. Machine-stitch over ends of handles several times to secure in place as shown in Figure 11.

Lining & Finishing the Bag

Step 1. Using the quilted bag top as a pattern, cut a lining piece from green print.

Step 2. Place lining piece right sides together with quilted top. Stitch across top edge of bag, stitching over handle ends.

Step 3. Press seam toward lining and topstitch close to seam on lining side as shown in Figure 12.

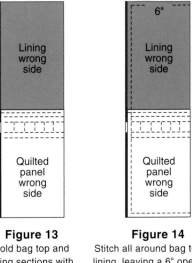

Figure 12
Press seam toward lining
and topstitch close to
seam on lining side.

Step 4. Fold bag top and lining sections with right sides together as shown in Figure 13. Starting at the bag bottom corner, stitch all around bag top and lining, leaving a 6" opening in the bottom edge of the lining as shown in Figure 14.

Figure 13
Fold bag top and
lining sections with
right sides together.

Figure 14
Stitch all around bag top and
lining, leaving a 6" opening in
the bottom edge of the lining.

Step 5. Trim corners of bag top and lining and trim batting close to seam at top side edge and along bottom corners to reduce bulk.

Step 6. Turn right side out through opening in lining, making sure corners are completely turned.

Step 7. Press seam inside at lining opening edges and machine-stitch opening closed close to edges as shown in Figure 15.

Figure 15
Press seam inside at opening
edges and machine-stitch
opening closed close to edges.

Step 8. Before inserting lining inside bag, press side seam of bag to help make bag lie flat at sides when complete.

Step 9. Insert lining inside bag. Press lining to the inside at the top edge of the bag. Insert iron inside bag and press lining flat as far inside as the iron will slide. Hold the top side of the bag and insert your hand inside the bag to the corners to be sure lining is completely inside and aligned at corners.

Step 10. Topstitch along top edge of bag ¼"–⅜" from top edge using matching all-purpose thread.

Step 11. Choose another area on the bag band and machine-quilt to hold lining layer and bag top together.

Note: This may be in the seam of a strip or ¼" from a seam or in the center of a strip. ❄

Santa Gift Bag
Placement Diagram
17½" x 21½"

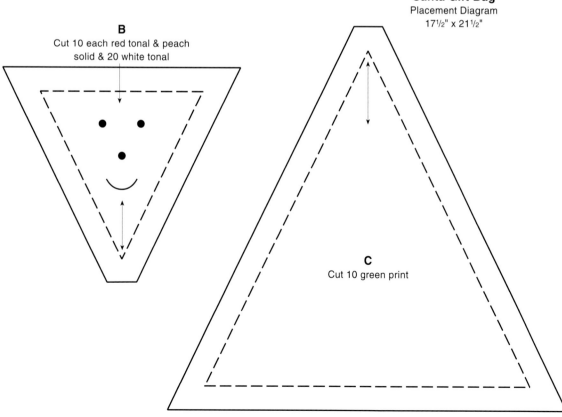

B
Cut 10 each red tonal & peach
solid & 20 white tonal

C
Cut 10 green print

Quilt a Colorful Christmas **155**

Oh, Christmas Tree

Use lots of scraps to make this pretty pieced tree design.

Project Specifications
Skill Level: Beginner
Quilt Size: 32" x 44"

Materials
- ⅛ yard total gold tonal scraps
- ⅛ yard total brown tonal scraps
- ¼ yard white tonal for borders
- ¾ yard red mottled for borders and binding
- ¾ yard total green tonal scraps
- 1 yard total white/cream tonal scraps
- Backing 38" x 52"
- Batting 38" x 52"
- All-purpose thread to match fabrics
- Quilting thread
- Basic sewing tools and supplies

Cutting
Step 1. Cut (124) 2⅞" x 2⅞" A squares white/cream tonal scraps; draw a line from corner to corner on the wrong side of 69 squares.

Step 2. Cut four 2⅞" x 2⅞" B squares brown tonal scraps; draw a line from corner to corner on the wrong side of two squares.

Step 3. Cut (96) 2⅞" x 2⅞" C squares green tonal scraps; draw a line from corner to corner on the wrong side of 42 squares.

Step 4. Cut eight 2⅞" x 2⅞" D squares gold tonal scraps; draw a line from corner to corner on the wrong side of three squares.

Step 5. Cut two 1½" x 24½" F strips and four 1½" x 36½" H strips white tonal.

Step 6. Cut four 2" x 24½" E strips and two 2" x 36½" G strips red mottled.

Step 7. Cut four 2¼" by fabric width strips red mottled for binding.

Piecing the Units
Step 1. To piece an A-A unit, referring to Figure 1, place a marked A right sides together with an unmarked A; stitch ¼" on each side of the marked line. Cut apart on the marked line; press seam to one side on each unit. Repeat 55 times to make 110 A-A units.

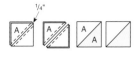

Figure 1
Complete A-A
units as shown.

Step 2. Referring to Figure 2, repeat Step 1 with four D squares to make four D-D units, three each D and A squares to make six A-D units, one each D and C squares to make two C-D units, four B squares to make four B-B units, 11 each C and A squares to make 22 A-C units and 84 C squares to make 84 C-C units.

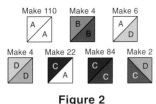

Figure 2
Complete units as shown.

Completing the Top

Step 1. Arrange and join the pieced units in rows referring to Figure 3, and number row sequence; press seams in adjacent rows in opposite directions.

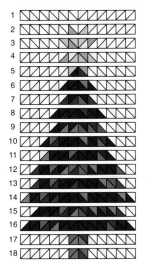

Figure 3
Join the pieced units in
rows, and number.

Step 2. Join the rows in numbered sequence; press seams in one direction.

Step 3. Sew an H strip between two G strips; repeat for two G-H-G strips. Press seams toward G. Repeat with F between two E strips to make two E-F-E strips.

Step 4. Sew G-H-G strips to opposite long sides of the pieced center; press seams toward strips.

Step 5. Join four B-B units to make a corner unit as shown in Figure 4; press seams in one direction.

Figure 4
Join 4 C-C units to
make a corner unit.

Step 6. Sew a B corner unit to the ends of an E-F-E strip; press seams toward E-F-E. Repeat for two strips.

Step 7. Sew a strip to the top and bottom of the pieced center; press seams toward strips.

Finishing the Quilt

Step 1. Sandwich batting between the completed top and prepared backing; pin or baste to hold layers together.

Step 2. Quilt as desired by hand or machine; remove pins or basting.

Step 3. When quilting is complete, trim batting and backing even with quilt top.

Step 4. Join the binding strips on short ends to make one long strip. Fold the strip in half along length with wrong sides together; press.

Step 5. Sew binding to quilt edges, mitering corners and overlapping ends. Fold binding to the backside and stitch in place. ❋

Oh, Christmas Tree
Placement Diagram
32" x 44"

Holly & Berry Runner

Make this runner tonight and use it on your table tomorrow.

Project Specifications

Skill Level: Beginner
Runner Size: 34" x 16"
Block Size: 8" x 8"
Number of Blocks: 3

Materials

- Scrap green/red print
- 1/8 yard red tonal
- 1/4 yard red mottled
- 1/3 yard tan tonal
- 1/2 yard black holly print
- Backing 38" x 20"
- Batting 38" x 20"
- All-purpose thread to match fabrics
- Quilting thread
- 1/4 yard fusible web
- Basic sewing tools and supplies

Cutting

Step 1. Cut one 8½" by fabric width strip tan tonal; subcut strip into three 8½" A squares. Fold and crease A to mark center.

Step 2. Cut four 1½" x 8½" B strips and two 1½" x 26½" C strips red mottled.

Step 3. Cut four 1½" x 1½" D squares green/red print.

Step 4. Cut two 3½" x 28½" E strips and two 3½" x 10½" G strips black holly print.

Step 5. Cut four 3½" x 3½" F squares red tonal.

Step 6. Cut three 2¼" by fabric width strips black holly print for binding.

Holly & Berry
8" x 8" Block

Appliquéing the Blocks

Step 1. Prepare templates for appliqué shapes using patterns given; trace shapes onto the paper side of the fusible web as directed on patterns for number to cut.
Note: *Patterns are given in reverse for fusible appliqué.*

Step 2. Cut out shapes, leaving a margin around each one. Fuse shapes to the wrong side of the fabrics as directed on patterns for color.

Step 3. Cut out shapes on traced lines; remove paper backing.

Step 4. Center a holly/berry motif on an A square in numerical order referring to the pattern; fuse shapes in place. Repeat for three blocks.

Step 5. Using all-purpose thread to match fabrics, machine satin-stitch around shapes to complete the blocks.

Completing the Top

Step 1. Join the three blocks with four B strips referring to the Placement Diagram for positioning of blocks. Press seams toward B.

Step 2. Sew a D square to each end of each C strip; press seams toward C.

Step 3. Sew a C-D strip to opposite sides of the pieced center; press seams toward C-D strips.

Step 4. Sew an E strip to opposite long sides of the pieced center; press seams toward E.

Step 5. Sew an F square to each end of each G strip; press seams toward G.

Step 6. Sew an F-G strip to opposite short ends of the pieced center; press seams toward F-G strips to complete the top.

Finishing the Quilt

Step 1. Sandwich batting between the completed top and prepared backing; pin or baste to hold layers together.

Step 2. Quilt as desired by hand or machine; remove pins or basting.

Step 3. When quilting is complete, trim batting and backing even with quilt top.

Step 4. Join the binding strips on short ends to make one long strip. Fold the strip in half along length with wrong sides together; press.

Step 5. Sew binding to quilt edges, mitering corners and overlapping ends. Fold binding to the back side and stitch in place. ❄

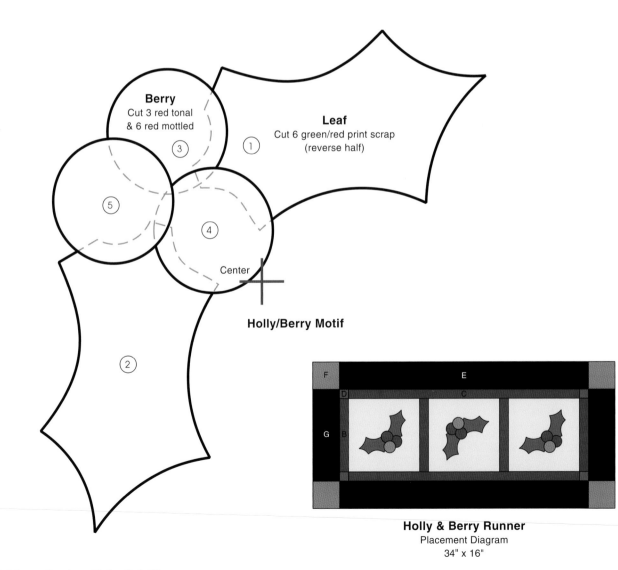

Berry
Cut 3 red tonal
& 6 red mottled

Leaf
Cut 6 green/red print scrap
(reverse half)

③
①
⑤
④
②

Center

Holly/Berry Motif

Holly & Berry Runner
Placement Diagram
34" x 16"

Christmas Cottage Pomegranate

Appliqué pomegranate shapes make a lovely holiday runner.

Project Specifications
Skill Level: Beginner
Runner Size: 36" x 16"
Block Size: 9" x 9"
Number of Blocks: 3

Materials
- Scraps medium and dark red tonals
- ¼ yard green tonal
- ¼ yard green/red print for binding
- ⅓ yard cream tonal
- ⅓ yard red mottled
- Backing 40" x 20"
- Batting 40" x 20"
- All-purpose thread to match fabrics
- Quilting thread
- ¼ yard fusible web
- Basic sewing tools and supplies

Cutting
Step 1. Cut one 9½" by fabric width strip cream tonal; subcut into three 9½" A squares. Fold and crease each square to mark the diagonal centers.
Step 2. Cut two 1½" x 9½" B sashing strips green tonal.
Step 3. Cut two 4" x 9½" C strips and two 4" x 29½" D strips red mottled.

Pomegranate
9" x 9" Block

Step 4. Cut four 4" x 4" E squares green tonal.
Step 5. Cut three 2¼" by fabric width strips green/red print for binding.

Appliquéing the Blocks
Step 1. Prepare templates for appliqué shapes using pattern given; trace three of each shape onto the paper side of the fusible web.
Step 2. Cut out shapes, leaving a margin around each one. Fuse shapes to the wrong side of the fabrics as directed on patterns for color.
Step 3. Cut out shapes on traced lines; remove paper backing.
Step 4. Arrange one floral motif on the diagonal of an A square in numerical order referring to the pattern; fuse shapes in place. Repeat for three blocks.

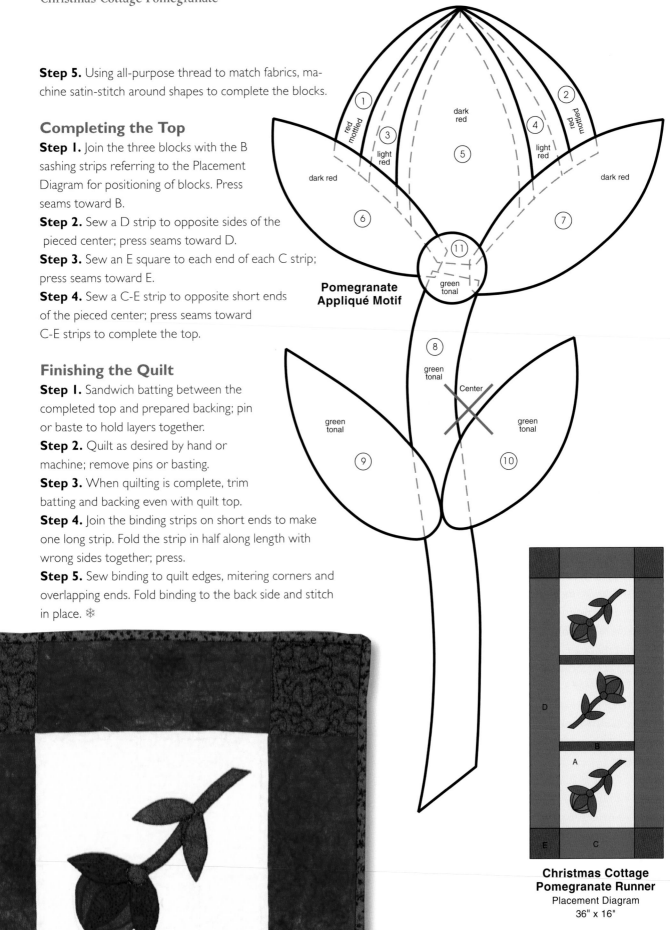

Christmas Cottage Pomegranate

Step 5. Using all-purpose thread to match fabrics, machine satin-stitch around shapes to complete the blocks.

Completing the Top

Step 1. Join the three blocks with the B sashing strips referring to the Placement Diagram for positioning of blocks. Press seams toward B.

Step 2. Sew a D strip to opposite sides of the pieced center; press seams toward D.

Step 3. Sew an E square to each end of each C strip; press seams toward E.

Step 4. Sew a C-E strip to opposite short ends of the pieced center; press seams toward C-E strips to complete the top.

Finishing the Quilt

Step 1. Sandwich batting between the completed top and prepared backing; pin or baste to hold layers together.

Step 2. Quilt as desired by hand or machine; remove pins or basting.

Step 3. When quilting is complete, trim batting and backing even with quilt top.

Step 4. Join the binding strips on short ends to make one long strip. Fold the strip in half along length with wrong sides together; press.

Step 5. Sew binding to quilt edges, mitering corners and overlapping ends. Fold binding to the back side and stitch in place. ❈

Pomegranate Appliqué Motif

red mottled
dark red
light red
①
③
⑤
④
②
light red
red mottled
dark red
dark red
⑥
⑦
⑪
green tonal
⑧
green tonal
Center
green tonal
green tonal
⑨
⑩

Christmas Cottage Pomegranate Runner
Placement Diagram
36" x 16"

D
B
A
E
C

Wreath Quartet Topper

Four simple pieced blocks make up this easy holiday table topper.

Project Specifications
Skill Level: Beginner
Quilt Size: 32½" x 32½"
Block Size: 12½" x 12½"
Number of Blocks: 4

Materials
- ⅙ yard each 9 greens
- ⅓ yard green print
- ⅜ yard red tonal
- ⅔ yard cream tonal
- Backing 37" x 37"
- Batting 37" x 37"
- All-purpose thread to match fabrics
- Quilting thread
- Basic sewing tools and supplies

Cutting
Step 1. Cut four 3" by fabric width strips cream tonal; subcut three strips into (15) 8" A pieces. Subcut the remaining strip into one 8" A piece and eight 3" D squares.
Step 2. Cut two 3⅜" by fabric width strips cream tonal; subcut strips into (16) 3⅜" squares. Cut each square in half on one diagonal to make B triangles.
Step 3. Cut four 3" by fabric width strips red tonal; subcut one strip into five 8" G pieces, one strip into four 5½" H pieces and six 3" I squares, one strip into six 3" I squares and one 21" F strip. Cut the fourth strip into two 21" F strips.

Step 4. Cut a 3" x 21" E strip from six of the greens.
Step 5. Cut a 3⅜" x 21" strip from each of the remaining greens. Subcut one of the strips into six 3⅜" squares and each of the remaining two strips into five 3⅜" squares. Cut each square in half on one diagonal to make 32 C triangles.
Step 6. Cut four 2¼" by fabric width strips green print for binding.

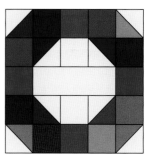

Wreath
12½" x 12½" Block

Piecing the Blocks
Step 1. To piece one block, sew B to C to make a B-C unit; press seams toward C. Repeat for eight units.
Step 2. Sew a B-C unit to opposite sides of D as shown in Figure 1; press seams toward D; repeat for two units.
Step 3. Sew a B-C-D unit to opposite sides of A, again referring to Figure 1; press seams toward A.
Step 4. Sew an F strip between two E strips with right sides together along length; press seams toward F. Repeat for three strip sets.
Step 5. Subcut the E-F strip sets into (16) 3" E-F units as shown in Figure 2.

Figure 1
Sew a B-C-D unit to opposite sides of A.

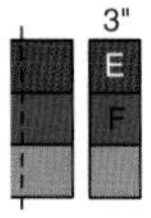

Figure 2
Subcut the E-F strip
sets into 3" E-F units.

Figure 3
Sew an E-F unit to opposite
sides of the B-C-D-A unit.

Step 6. Referring to Figure 3, sew an E-F unit to opposite sides of the B-C-D-A unit; press seams toward E-F.

Step 7. Sew a B-C unit to opposite ends of an E-F unit as shown in Figure 4; repeat for two units. Press seams toward the E-F units.

Figure 4
Sew a B-C unit to
opposite ends of
an E-F unit.

Step 8. Sew a B-C-E-F unit to the top and bottom of the previously pieced center unit to complete one block; repeat for four blocks. Press seams away from block center.

Completing the Top

Step 1. Sew I to each end of A; press seams toward I. Repeat for two A-I units.

Step 2. Join two blocks with an A-I unit to make a block row; press seams toward A-I units. Repeat for two block rows.

Step 3. Sew G between two A pieces and add I to each end as shown in Figure 5; press seams toward G and I. Repeat for three pieced strips.

Figure 5
Sew G between 2 A pieces
and add I to each end.

Step 4. Join the block rows with a pieced strip as shown in Figure 6; press seams toward pieced strip.

Step 5. Sew a pieced strip to the top and bottom of the pieced center, press seams toward strips.

Step 6. Join two A and two H pieces with G to make a strip as shown in Figure 7; press seams toward H and G. Repeat for two strips.

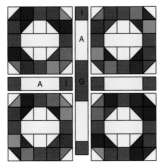

Figure 6
Join the block rows
with the pieced strips.

Step 7. Sew a strip to the opposite sides of the pieced center, again referring to Figure 7, to complete the pieced top. Press seams toward strips.

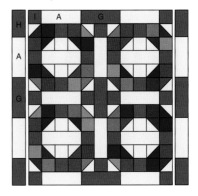

Figure 7
Join strips with pieced center as shown.

Finishing the Quilt

Step 1. Sandwich batting between the completed top and prepared backing; pin or baste to hold layers together.

Step 2. Quilt as desired by hand or machine; remove pins or basting.

Step 3. When quilting is complete, trim batting and backing even with quilt top.

Step 4. Join the binding strips on short ends to make one long strip. Fold the strip in half along length with wrong sides together; press.

Step 5. Sew binding to quilt edges, mitering corners and overlapping ends. Fold binding to the back side and stitch in place. ❄

Wreath Quartet Topper
Placement Diagram
32½" x 32½"

DESIGN BY **CHRISTINE SCHULTZ**

Dancing Stars Tree Skirt

Octagonal star-design blocks dance around this splendid tree skirt.

Project Specifications

Skill Level: Advanced
Quilt Size: Approximately 43" x 43"
Block Size: 14" x 12"
Number of Blocks: 6

Materials

- ⅝ yard each red and white prints
- ⅝ yard medium green tonal
- 2 yards black print
- Backing 49" x 49"
- Batting 49" x 49"
- All-purpose thread to match fabrics
- Quilting thread
- Basic sewing tools and supplies

Instructions

Step 1. Prepare templates using pattern pieces given; cut as directed on each piece.

Step 2. Join one each A, B and C pieces in colors shown in Figure 1 to complete units. Repeat for nine of each unit. Press seams away from A.

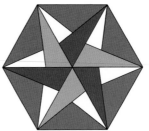

Dancing Star
14" x 12" Block

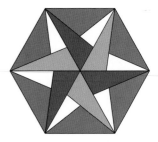

Dancing Star Reversed
14" x 12" Block

Step 3. Join one Unit 4 with two Unit 1's as shown in Figure 2; repeat for three 1-4-1 units. Press seams toward C.

Figure 2
Complete 1-4-1 units as shown.

Figure 3
Complete 4-1-4 units as shown.

Step 4. Join one Unit 1 with two Unit 4's as shown in Figure 3; repeat for three 4-1-4 units. Press seams toward C.

Step 5. Join a 1-4-1 unit with a 4-1-4 unit to complete one Dancing Star block as shown in Figure 4. Press seam toward C.

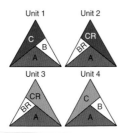

Figure 1
Complete units as shown.

Figure 4
Join units to complete a block.

Step 6. Repeat Steps 3–5 to make a Dancing Star Reversed block using Units 2 and 3 as shown in Figure 5; press seams toward CR.

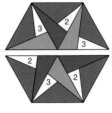

Figure 5
Join units to complete a
reversed block.

Step 7. Sew D to one side of each block as shown in Figure 6; press seams toward D.

Make 3   Make 3

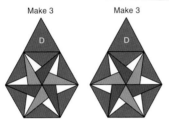

Figure 6
Sew D to 1 side of each block.

Step 8. Join three pieced units to make a half unit as shown in Figure 7, alternating blocks and reversed blocks; press seams in one direction. Repeat for two half units.

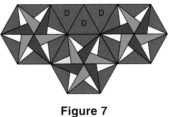

Figure 7
Join 3 pieced units,
alternating blocks.

Step 9. Join the two half units, leaving one seam open from center to outer edge; press seams in one direction.

Step 10. Set E into outer edges between blocks and ½ E and ½ ER at opening ends as shown in Figure 8. Press seams toward E pieces.

Step 11. Add F, G and half pieces, again referring to Figure 8; press pieces toward F and G pieces.

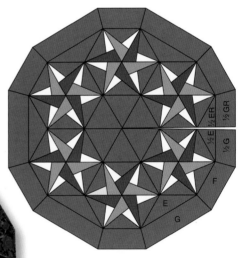

Figure 8
Add E, F and G pieces and
half pieces as shown.

Step 12. Make a 3" circle template of plastic or cardboard; mark a circle around the center of the pieced top.

Step 13. Sandwich batting between the completed top and prepared backing; pin or baste to hold layers together.

Step 14. Quilt as desired by hand or machine; remove pins or basting; do not quilt inside the circle area.

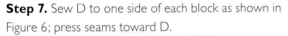

Note: *The quilting design used in the outer-edge pieces is given.*

Step 15. When quilting is complete, trim batting and backing even with quilt top.

Step 16. Cut just inside the marked center circle line; stay-stitch ⅛" from cut edge.

Step 17. Cut five 2½" by fabric width strips black print for binding; set aside one strip for circle opening. Join the remaining strips on short ends to make one long strip.

Figure 9
Stitch ends of tails and along
folded edge of tail as shown.

Step 18. Sew longer binding piece to all edges except inside circle. Fold binding to the back side and stitch in place. Repeat on inside circle, centering the remaining binding strip in the center of the unopened sides of the center circle, leaving the remaining tail at each end for tying. Fold the ends of the tail pieces to the inside; stitch along open edges of tails as shown in Figure 9 to complete. ❋

Dancing Stars Tree Skirt
Placement Diagram
Approximately 43" x 43"

B
Cut 36 white print
(reverse half for BR)

A
Cut 36 black print

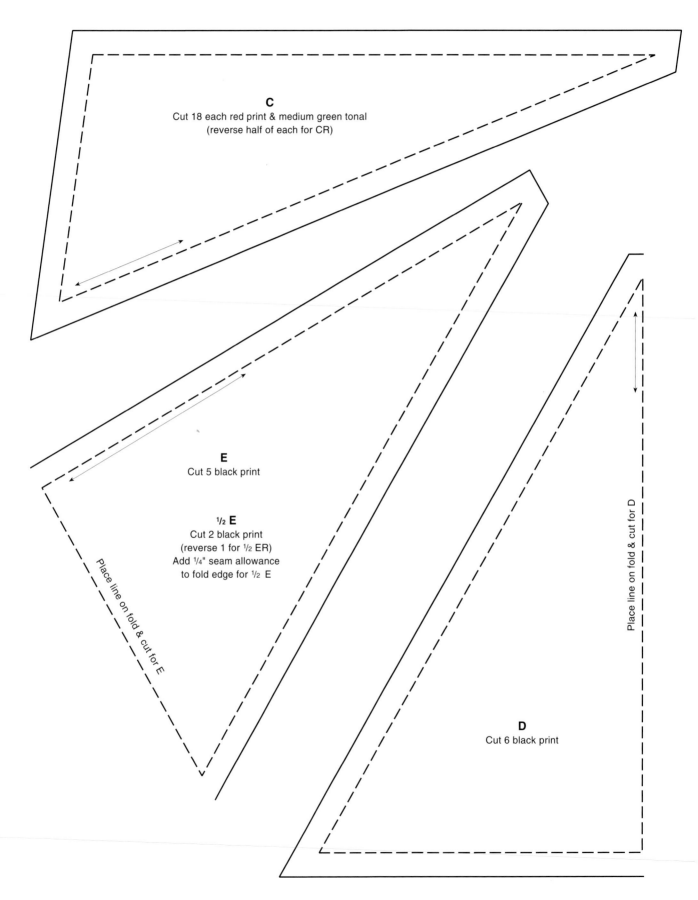

C
Cut 18 each red print & medium green tonal
(reverse half of each for CR)

E
Cut 5 black print

½ E
Cut 2 black print
(reverse 1 for ½ ER)
Add ¼" seam allowance
to fold edge for ½ E

Place line on fold & cut for E

Place line on fold & cut for D

D
Cut 6 black print

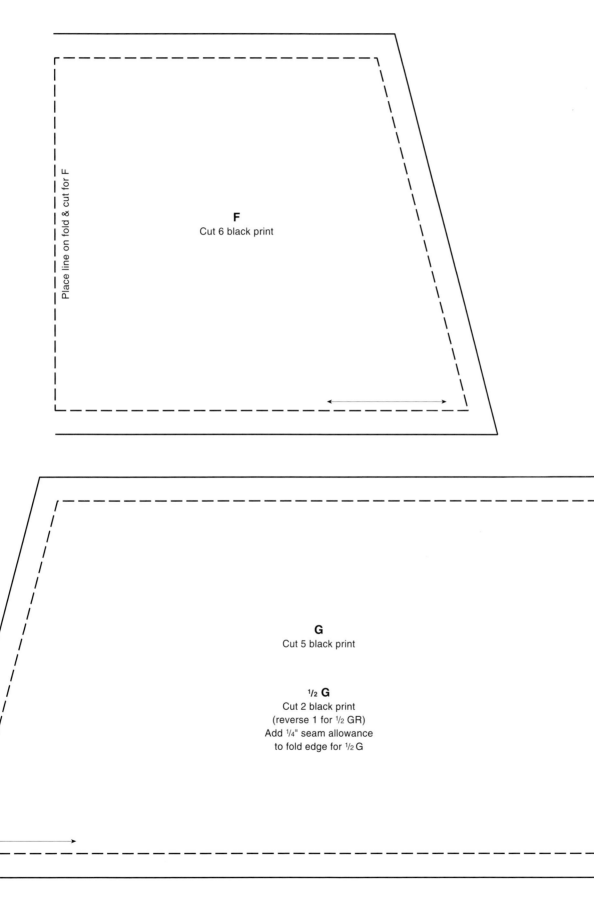

Place line on fold & cut for F

F
Cut 6 black print

G
Cut 5 black print

½ G
Cut 2 black print
(reverse 1 for ½ GR)
Add ¼" seam allowance
to fold edge for ½ G

Place line on fold & cut for G

Quilting Design

Metric Conversion Charts

Standard Equivalents

U.S. Measurement		Metric Measurement		
1/8 inch	=	3.20 mm	=	0.32 cm
1/4 inch	=	6.35 mm	=	0.635 cm
3/8 inch	=	9.50 mm	=	0.95 cm
1/2 inch	=	12.70 mm	=	1.27 cm
5/8 inch	=	15.90 mm	=	1.59 cm
3/4 inch	=	19.10 mm	=	1.91 cm
7/8 inch	=	22.20 mm	=	2.22 cm
1 inch	=	25.40 mm	=	2.54 cm
1/8 yard	=	11.43 cm	=	0.11 m
1/4 yard	=	22.86 cm	=	0.23 m
3/8 yard	=	34.29 cm	=	0.34 m
1/2 yard	=	45.72 cm	=	0.46 m
5/8 yard	=	57.15 cm	=	0.57 m
3/4 yard	=	68.58 cm	=	0.69 m
7/8 yard	=	80.00 cm	=	0.80 m
1 yard	=	91.44 cm	=	0.91 m

Metric Conversions

U.S. Measurements		Multiplied by		Metric Measurement
yards	×	.9144	=	meters (m)
yards	×	91.44	=	centimeters (cm)
inches	×	2.54	=	centimeters (cm)
inches	×	25.40	=	millimeters (mm)
inches	×	.0254	=	meters (m)

Metric Measurements		Multiplied by		U.S. Measurements
centimeters	×	.3937	=	inches
meters	×	1.0936	=	yards

Embroidery Stitch Guide

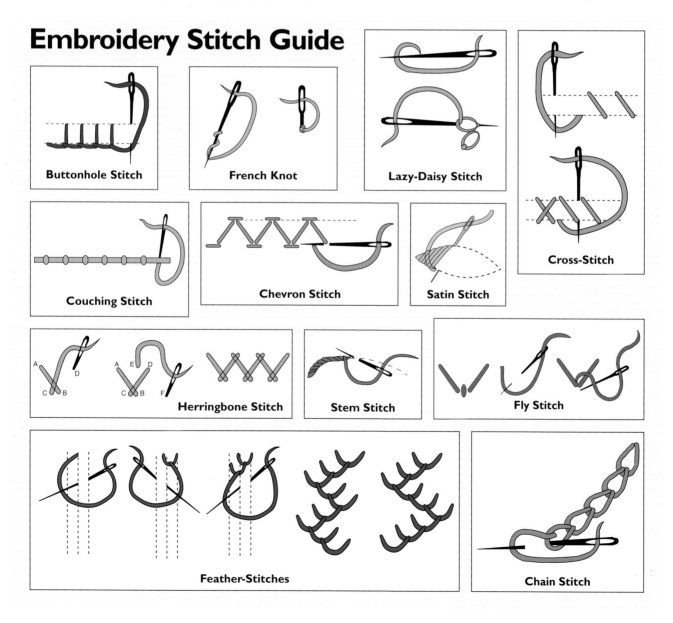

Buttonhole Stitch

French Knot

Lazy-Daisy Stitch

Cross-Stitch

Couching Stitch

Chevron Stitch

Satin Stitch

Herringbone Stitch

Stem Stitch

Fly Stitch

Feather-Stitches

Chain Stitch

Special Thanks

We would like to thank the talented quilt designers whose work is featured in this collection.

Barbara Clayton
Fancy Holly Table
   Runner, 123
French Horn Place Mat, 78
Friendly Snowman
   Tree Skirt, 137
Red & White Christmas, 9

**Lucy Fazely &
Michael L. Burns**
Christmas Dreams, 7
Connecting Wreaths, 51
Kaleidoscope Stars, 16

Sandra L. Hatch
Christmas Swirls, 54
Santa Gift Bag, 151
Snowman Surprise, 33

Paula Jeffery
Quilty Santa, 58

Connie Kauffman
Crazy Christmas Tree, 143
Mother & Child, 73
Winter Snowfall, 37

Pearl Louise Krush
Christmas Cottage
   Pomegranate, 163
Holly & Berry Runner, 159
Log Cabin Mantel
   Cover, 75

Toby Lischko
Reindeer Tracks, 133
Stairway to the Stars, 21

Chris Malone
Denim Pals, 86
Quilter's Ornaments, 147

Connie Rand
Christmas Flowers, 90
Starry Christmas Night, 28

Judith Sandstrom
Christmas Jewels, 25
Visions of Snowmen, 40
Wreath Quartet Topper, 165

Christine Schultz
Dancing Stars Tree
   Skirt, 168
Light of the World, 100
Sampler Christmas
   Stocking, 94

Karla Schulz
Christmas Puzzle, 105
Homespun Christmas, 47

Marian Shenk
Holly Jolly Basket, 109

Willow Ann Sirch
Holly & Ivy Flannel Throw, 62
Vintage Patchwork
   Stocking, 118
Wreath of Plenty, 114

Jodi Warner
Holly Swirls, 66

Julie Weaver
Blooming Christmas, 83
Holly, Wood & Vine, 129
Oh, Christmas Tree, 156

Fabrics & Supplies

Page 7: Christmas Dreams—Holiday Palette fabric collection from Classic Cottons, Steam-A-Seam 2 double-stick fusible web and Warm & Natural cotton batting from The Warm Co., 6½" x 24" ruler from Quilter's Rule, Coats Dual Duty Plus all purpose, transparent nylon monofilament and Star Multi Color Quilting & Craft Thread and Sullivan's Quilt Basting Spray used to make sample. Stitched on a Pfaff Creative 2144.

Page 16: Kaleidoscope Stars— Holiday Palette fabric collection from Classic Cottons, Steam-A-Seam 2 Double Stick Fusible Web and Warm & Natural cotton batting from The Warm Co., Quilter's Rule 6½" x 24" ruler, Coats Dual Duty Plus all purpose, transparent nylon monofilament and Star Multi Color Quilting & Craft Thread and Sullivan's Quilt Basting Spray used to make

sample. Stitched on a Pfaff Creative 2144.

Page 25: Christmas Jewels—Hobbs Heirloom Premium cotton batting, Fiskars rotary-cutting tools and DMC quilting thread and needles.

Page 33: Snowman Surprise—Star Machine Quilting and Craft Thread from Coats and Cotton Classic batting from Fairfield Processing. Machine-quilted by Dianne Hodgkins.

Page 37: Winter Snowfall—Steam-A-Seam 2 from The Warm Co.

Page 40: Visions of Snowmen—Wonder-Under fusible web, Hobbs Heirloom cotton batting, Fiskars rotary-cutting tools and DMC quilting thread and needles.

Page 47: Homespun Christmas—Warm & Natural cotton batting from The Warm Co., #4107 Antique Christmas quilting thread

from Sulky Blendables and Golden Threads Winger Earthlines quilting designs by Julie Mullin.

Page 51: Connecting Wreaths—Holiday Palette fabrics from Classic Cottons, Warm & Natural cotton batting from The Warm Co., 6½" x 24" ruler from Quilter's Rule, basting spray from Sullivan's USA Inc. and Coats Dual Duty Plus all-purpose and Star Multi Color Quilting & Craft Thread from Coats used to make sample. Sample stitched on a Pfaff Creative 2144.

Page 54: Christmas Swirls—Deck the Halls fabric collection from RJR, Cotton Classic batting from Fairfield Processing and Star Machine Quilting & Craft Thread from Coats. Machine-quilted by Dianne Hodgkins.

Page 62: Holly & Ivy Flannel Throw—Magic Sizing spray.

Page 73: Mother & Child— Steam-A-Seam 2 fusible web

from The Warm Co., Sulky silver metallic thread and Hobbs Heirloom fusible batting.

Page 78: French Horn Place Mat—Pellon interfacing.

Page 83: Blooming Christmas—Christmas Presence flannel from Maywood Studio.

Page 109: Holly Jolly Basket—Heat & Bond fusible web from The Warm Co. and Unique Stitch fabric glue.

Page 114: Wreath of Plenty—Magic Sizing spray.

Page 133: Reindeer Tracks—RJR Thimbleberries fabrics and Quilter's Dream cotton batting.

Page 143: Crazy Christmas Tree—Steam-A-Seam 2 Lite from The Warm Co. and gold metallic thread from Sulky.

Page 156: Oh, Christmas Tree—Warm & Natural Batting from The Warm Co.